BETWEEN THE LINES

Steppenwolf's Seagull
and a
Reluctant Actor's Journey
Back to the Stage

Eric Simonson

For Sue and Henry

First published in 2024

Library of Congress Cataloguing-in-Publishing Data|
Simonson, Eric, 1960—
Between the Lines: A Reluctant Actor's Journey Back to the Stage / Eric Simonson

ISBN 978-1-959457-22-0 (paperback)
1. Simonson, Eric 1949— — Diaries. 2. Chekhov, Anton, 1860—1904. Seagull. 3. Steppenwolf Theatre Company. 4. The Grapes of Wrath. 6. Actors. 7. Chicago Theatre.

Published by Blue Jay Ink, Ojai, California

Printed in the United States of America

Prologue

"He wiped his face with the towel again. 'Old man, a book can have Chicago in it, and not be about Chicago. It can have a tennis player in it without being about a tennis player.'
I didn't get it. I probably looked it, for he went on, 'Take this book here, old man—' and he held up one of the books he had swiped from some library. Along with the numbers I could see Hemingway's name on the spine. 'There's a prizefighter in it, old man, but it's not about a prizefighter.'
'Is it about the sun rising?' I said. I knew that was part of the title.
'Goddam if I know what it's about,' he said...'"

— Wright Morris, *The Huge Season*

NOT LONG AGO, I found myself in Appleton, Wisconsin, giving a lecture at my alma mater, Lawrence University, about my adventures writing for television. I talked about what I thought it took to get an idea for a series on the air, and I told stories about all the funny and interesting people I had met along the way as I traversed the impossible minefield of the Hollywood entertainment machine. Despite the endless gatekeepers I had come up against and the impossible odds of getting a show on the air, I really did love my job as a television writer, and I think that came across in my talk. But somewhere along the way—I think I was discussing

something about working outside one's comfort zone—I mentioned I had just finished a stint acting live on stage at Steppenwolf
Theatre, in a production of Anton Chekhov's *Seagull*. And to boot,
I had done this after being off the stage for more than three decades. Then I moved on to more talk about writers' rooms and series
I admired, etc. And after I had finished, I opened the floor up to
questions. A bunch of hands flew up and I picked the first person
I saw, who asked, "What was it like to act on stage after being away
from it for so long?"

Okay, not a question related to the general gist of my talk, but
fair enough. And I answered.

Next question: "How do you feel about it now—I mean the
acting thing? Would you ever do it again?"

And so it went. More talk about acting, getting back on stage
and managing my chronic stage fright. We did eventually get back
to the subject of television, but the interest in my brief and not
so brilliant return to the stage was to be the start of a trend. For
weeks, and then months afterwards — to this day even—I can
talk to anyone about a number of projects I am working on (and I
work on a lot of different things at the same time) but the one thing
people seem most people interested in is me, on stage, playing Dr.
Dorn in *Seagull* at Steppenwolf Theatre.

I'm not sure if this is because people see me as a 60-something
amateur actor, or if they are more curious about a person quitting acting at an early age and then getting back on the boards
decades later. Perhaps it's a little of both. But the questions came
up—comes up—so frequently that I thought I might write a little
article about the experience and, if I was lucky, get it published
in some trade publication like *American Theatre Magazine*. Or

maybe I'd just post it online, I don't know. Acting in *Seagull* was, after all, one of the most terrifying experiences of my life.

So I put pen to paper and, as I did, a whole slew of other thoughts and memories came flooding back, about acting, writing, directing, and theater in general. And gradually the magazine idea grew into something, well, a lot longer than just an article.

Returning to acting also meant returning to Steppenwolf, where I am a company member, and Chicago, where I started as a young artist trying to make my way in, around, and through what turned out to be the golden age of Chicago theater. I had little training when I graduated from Lawrence and moved to Chicago, where I found scores of actors with a whole range of different kinds of backgrounds and experience. But that didn't seem to matter to anyone wanting to make it in off-loop or off-off-loop theater Chicago was the great leveling field. Anyone could make it, and most of us were all there to learn by doing. And we were there because word had gotten out—there was a gold rush of great theater going on in Chicago and we all wanted to be a part of it. Chicago theater was our apprenticeship. We were cutting our teeth at a time and in a place that was rethinking what theater was, what acting was, and how a community of audiences and artists might come together and make something new and special for one another.

Some may take issue with me calling the years between 1980 and 1995 the golden age of Chicago theater (and also the fact that those were the same approximate years I happened to be in Chicago), and I don't mean to disparage anything that came before or since. Of course there have been many triumphs on the other side of these 15 years. All the same, I do think I can make a case for the immediacy of that time, when the sky was the limit for anyone wanting something irreverent, cutting edge and exciting.

So in the following pages, which started out as a meditation of an actor returning to the stage, I have interspersed memories about how I came to this place in my life, and how early experiences in Chicago with extraordinary people came to shape me as an artist. And as a person.

This hodgepodge of thoughts and memories, this cool, limp lima bean of a book, is what materialized. It's a weird, kind of Frankenstein reminiscence, part memoir, part journal. Not really one or the other, and not necessarily a mash-up of both. But it's not unlike, I suppose, the series of books George Plimpton wrote in the 1960s and '70s, documenting his experiences as an amateur competing with and against pro athletes (as a quarterback, baseball pitcher and boxer).

This trip down memory surface streets has been more than rewarding to write, but I am well aware I am just one of many actors, playwrights, writers, backstage artists, designers who have had similar but uniquely different experiences. There are probably more interesting and more important stories from this period than mine. And people should tell those stories. I suppose I needed to get these thoughts out and also, in a way, say thanks to Chicago for shaping me into the artist I am today: some jamoke who learned just enough to make it in the entertainment business. The most valuable of Chicago theater lessons being this: go ahead and take a leap into the dark.

1

The Path Back

*"The questions Mrs. Daloney had raised, or failed to
answer, stuck in my mind like fish hooks which trailed
their broken lines into the past."*

— Ross MacDonald, *The Chill*

THE OFFER came in the form of an e-mail from Steppenwolf's
Casting Director J.C. Clementz. It read:

> *"As you know, the first subscription production in the new
> round theatre space will be Yasen Peyankov's adaptation
> of Seagull by Anton Chekhov. We know that you haven't
> acted in a while but thought it would be fun to ask. We
> would like to offer you the role of Yevgeny Dorn. You will
> find the script draft attached, and below are the dates."*

I stopped to lift my eyes from the laptop screen. There must be
some mistake, right? I am not an actor—I mean, I was, but that
was a long time ago. Ancient history.

I re-read the e-mail.

Nope, no mistake. This was a genuine offer. To play Yevgeny Sergeyevich Dorn in Anton Chekhov's *Seagull* at Steppenwolf Theatre, where I am a company member. But as a director and writer, not an actor. This was just, weird.

I thought about it. Then decided not to think about it for a while.

Then I sat on it for a couple more days to let it settle. I finally ran the offer past Sue, my wife, and she stared back blankly.

"Is it a joke?" she asked.

I hadn't thought of that. Perhaps it was. I called J.C., and he laughed. No joke, no such luck, they were dead serious.

He went on to explain that Steppenwolf was opening a brand new, multimillion dollar theater with this production of *Seagull*, and they were looking for as much ensemble participation as possible. That made sense. And as he spoke, the thought occurred to me it could not have been that easy, finding fifty-something actors to commit to a three month rehearsal and performance schedule, especially so soon after the pandemic.

My next call was to Yasen Payenkov, the author and director of the new adaption. He sort of chuckled at the thought of me getting an offer out of the blue, and mentioned the venture would be ironic, since I had recently directed *him* in a show I had written and directed myself.[1]

But Yasen had never seen me act before. How could he be sure I was any good, or for that matter, even right for the role? He admitted as much, but said he had an instinct this would be a good fit.

I told both him and J.C. I would have to think about it. This

---

1. *Lindiwe*, a play with music, and my third collaboration with the South African singing group Ladysmith Black Mambazo.

was quite a commitment, and not one to be taken lightly, because the last time I set foot on the stage—32 years prior—had been a disaster.

* * *

In late summer of 1990, when I was 30 years old, I left the Broadway cast of *The Grapes of Wrath,* happily I might add, to return to my first love, directing, back in Chicago at Steppenwolf Theatre. Randy Arney, the company's artistic director, had asked me if I would helm David Hare's play *The Secret Rapture.* The play had done poorly on Broadway and there was a bit of a dust up between Hare and *New York Times* chief critic, Frank Rich. Steppenwolf was given the rights to do the first ever production outside Broadway, and the hope was that Hare would be vindicated with a well received, new production at Steppenwolf. This was a plum assignment and a no-brainer as far as I was concerned. Getting to direct my first big equity show was a break I had been waiting years for. And acting had never been my first love. It was always a means to an end, and in fact, at that point in my life, I had come to despise practicing the craft.

When I first started out in theater, I had practically nothing. I moved to Chicago in 1983, age 21, fresh from Wisconsin. I had (literally) two hundred dollars in my pocket. My intention was to check out the then-burgeoning theater scene because, well, I couldn't think of anything else to do with my post-graduate self. And I didn't have any real options or plans. I had virtually no skills. I contemplated graduate school, but I was broke—or rather, in debt with college loans—and I wasn't convinced more education was my path anyway. And Chicago was calling, the secret was out. Theaters like Steppenwolf, Wisdom Bridge, Goodman, Organic, and Remains were coming into their own, making a national impact and sending fresh productions and new plays far and wide. Chicago theater was on the rise and, if the performing arts were indeed my path, I wanted to be a part of it all.

I was a director, or thought of myself as one. But I had no professional credits and came armed with nothing more than a little encouragement from one of my two theater professors, who told me he thought I "might make a pretty good director." That was it, that was about all I had. That and an arrogant feeling I might be even better than just "a pretty good director." But, as everyone knows, theater is a tough business—as tough as they come. So many try, so few succeed. And those who do, do so just barely, spending years in penury scraping by, struggling to make a living. And where do you start if you have no connections? The catch twenty-two, of course, for a director is that no one will hire you unless they've seen your work... and you can't show your work unless someone hires you.

But I had a plan, and it was this: audition for parts and get cast as an actor. There were literally hundreds of storefront, non-union theaters in Chicago at that time. I reasoned that if I got cast in a show, I would get to know a few people and use this as a calling card and get to where I really wanted to be: in the director's chair.

So I pretended to be an actor until I could convince everyone I was a pretty good director. Or at least until someone called me out for being a bad actor.

I knew enough about acting to know that you had to come to auditions with a headshot and resume. So, before I left for Chicago, I hired a family portrait photographer from Waukesha, Wisconsin (where I had been staying with my parents) and got a headshot, which looked exactly like what you might expect from a family portrait photographer from Waukesha, Wisconsin. I made Steve Carell in the key art from *The 40-Year-Old Virgin* look super cool. And my resume wasn't much better. I had maybe three or four credits (from college, the result of a little mercy casting). I padded the special skills section with things like "Juggles, rides a unicycle, plays the banjo" (all true). I had no guidance whatsoever. At the end of my senior year at Lawrence, a liberal arts college not used to theater majors, the university's Career Center handed me a copy *What Color is Your Parachute?* and wished me luck.

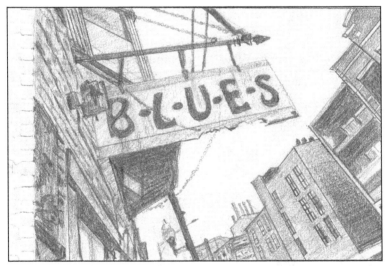

My first apartment in Chicago was on the third floor of a walk-up, above the popular the B.L.U.E.S. bar on North Halsted. I answered an ad in the Chicago Reader and shared the tiny three-bedroom with two strangers. Local blues legend Sarah "Big Time" Streeter lived on the second floor and we became friends. Every night I would fall asleep to the thumping bass lines of 'Sweet Home Chicago' and Caledonia.

Still, I wasn't a *bad* actor. I think. It's difficult to judge one-self. Arriving in Chicago, I remember lots of auditions and far too many rejections. I also remember a few small victories. Rummaging through the old memory box, I reminded myself I had a mixed success. This is from a production of a world premiere play called *Suffering Fools* by Chicago playwright Doug Post, who was experiencing a spate of local hit shows at the time. It was at The Commons Theatre, a well respected off-loop store-front (now defunct). I played the lead role of James, a ne'er-do-well, struggling writer who complained to just about anyone about everything. Tom Valeo, critic for the Chicago Reader, wrote this:

> *"Eric Simonson seems to drown in James's pompous and overblown speeches. [He] delivers them without affect, emphasizing James's depression."*

Ouch. Not the worst review, but certainly not good. And enough to bring any sensitive guy down for a good long while. Not that I never got a bad review outside of acting—I've had plenty as a writer and director—but a bad notice for an actor feels far more personal. Try reading what Valeo wrote and going out on stage the next night. I remember the pang of coming to the theatre the day after a bad notice, the stench of humiliation and doubt hanging in the air. Who among the cast had read those awful words? And what about the audience? Were they looking for the flaws called out by the reviewer? And would they allow it to affect their experience watching the play?

The answer to avoiding this angst, of course, is and always has been, never read reviews. But this was not an option for a young artist just starting out. I needed to test my mettle, see how I stood against the rest. And of course everything—my next job, my veritable future—depended on how I did on this particular job. Or so I thought. Everyone was watching and I needed a stamp of approval.

The thing is—and I would learn this gradually over the years— hardly anyone is watching. You think everyone is reading these reviews, but most folks have better things to do than check up on what the critics are saying about Eric Simonson's most recent performance.

Looking deeper into the memory box, on the other hand, there was some encouragement. This is from Richard Christiansen, the lead critic at the Chicago Tribune, reviewing a new play, *Blue Champagne*, premiering at Next Theatre (now defunct). I played the "good son" to a mother, played by Barbara June Patterson, who was in the middle of a red-lining crisis on the South Side of Chicago.[2]

> *"Both male participants are excellent: Eric Simonson as the decent, Ordinary Joe younger brother, and Terry Green, very fine in his South Side accent, as the rough young widower..."*

So I guess I wasn't bad. And at the time I was good enough to get cast in a few productions here and there. Besides Commons and Next, I worked at Free Shakespeare, Alliance and Lifeline Theatres. All of these except for Lifeline eventually went under. They went the way of 90% of these papier-mache Chicago operations—falling into non-production for a while and then quietly disappearing

---

2. Barbara June Patterson, at the time, was retired from Highland Park High School, where she had taught Jeff Perry and Gary Sinise. She is the reason these two met, and it's probably safe to say there would be no Steppenwolf Theatre if it were not for Barbara June Patterson. At the time I was acting in *Blue Champagne*, I knew none of this. Through the years, Jeff and Gary remained devoted to B.J.P. and never missed a chance to credit her with their success.

from the theater landscape altogether. Still, these theaters gave me, and hundreds of other folks, opportunities we would have never had otherwise. And at least one of them, Lifeline, thought I was pretty special. I'm not sure why, but they asked me to join their company less than a year after working with them, first as a light board operator and then as a house manager. I hadn't yet acted with the company, but they had seen me audition, and I guess they thought I had something. Or maybe they just needed another hand running the theatre and building sets. At any rate, they accepted me into their fold and gave me my first artistic home.

The Lifeline Theatre Ensemble, 1985. From left to right: Suzanne Plunkett, me, Kathy Sills, Meryl Friedman and Steve Totland. Photo: Tom Fezzey.

However fortunate I was to join Lifeline, though, the real goal for every actor in Chicago at that time was to get cast in a show at Steppenwolf, the storied artistic ensemble that had charmed and subdued critics with now folkloric productions like *True West* and *Balm in Gilead*. In the space of eight years, since its start in 1974, the theatre had launched the careers of John Malkovich, Laurie Metcalf, Joan Allen, and Gary Sinise. That caught people's attention. But the company had a reputation of being insular and hard to break into. They mostly drew from actors and theatre artists they knew, and administrative dealings were very secretive. At the time, the only way in for a fledgling actor was through the company's Educational Outreach Program, which sent skeletal productions around to local high schools. The company cast these shows with non-union actors outside the ensemble and paid them a little chump change, while the theatre satisfied educational outreach initiatives necessary to attract government grants. The venture, though, wasn't entirely mercenary. Some of the actors used in these productions actually graduated to main-stage shows, and the outreach program turned into a sort of farming system for the company.

But getting an audition for one of these productions was a nearly impossible feat. Steppenwolf would announce auditions and invite actors to call a phone line on a certain day and time. Within seconds, that phone line would jam for hours, and by the time one got through, there were a couple hundred people on the audition waiting list.

My opportunity to break this logger jam came when Lifeline cast Barbara "Boots" Irving, an amateur actor, in a play called *Touched*. I was also a part of that cast. Boots, a kind and enterprising woman in her sixties, was also Steppenwolf founding member Jeff Perry's aunt... and head of the company's Educational Outreach Program! I got to know Boots pretty well, as did the other actors in Lifeline, and—in the grand tradition of it's-not-what-you-know-but-who-you-know, she was more than happy to put our Lifeline names at the top of Steppenwolf's audition list, ahead of the call-in date. Around about that time, Steppenwolf was putting together a show called *From the Page to the Stage: A Shakespeare Sampler*, which was exactly as it sounds—an instructional collection of Shakespeare's "greatest hits" for high school students. I auditioned, made the final cut… and was rejected. I remember being inconsolable about this. My call-back audition had gone terribly. I was paired with Barb Prescott, an actor fresh out of DePaul's lauded theatre school, who was as nervous as I, and, for whatever reason, refused to run our scenes before we went in to read together. She wasn't just dismissive, she was downright hostile (we dated later of course). Nerves, I found out later. When we finally went in to read for casting director Phyllis Schuringa and director (and ensemble member) Tom Irwin, I remember I totally, unequivocally sucked. I tried my best but did not feel connected to the material. That might have been because I could sense Tom's interest was entirely on Barb. Which wasn't surprising. Barb was an excellent actor and definitely in the Steppenwolf vein of the balls-out acting style the company was known for. Regardless, I left that audition feeling completely defeated, knowing for certain I had failed.

I went straight to the apartment of my then girlfriend, Gina Pontillo, filled with despair. I was certain I had scuttled my big opportunity. I was inches away from crossing the finish line in first place and fell flat on my face. But Gina, who had this phenomenal, crazy sixth sense, wasn't convinced. I remember with great clarity the moment she told me, "This is not over." And like magic, sure enough, a couple days later, Phyllis called to say one of the actors had dropped out of the play, and I was being offered the part.

My first job at Steppenwolf — acting in From the Page to the Stage: a Shakespeare Sampler (1986). From left to right: Holly Wantuch, Barb Prescott and John C. Reilly. I've lost touch with the fellow standing next to me, and Steppenwolf has no record of the production (maybe it never happened)!

It was a miracle. There were hundreds of actors auditioning for only five spots, and I felt pretty damned lucky. It was a motley cast, which included Barb and a then unknown John C. Reilly. Together, we had little enthusiasm for the script or the production, and Tom Irwin seemed a little distracted. This was around 1985, and not every actor in the Steppenwolf ensemble was having the same success as Malkvovich and Metcalf. The ones who stayed behind in Chicago did all they could to supplement their subsistence wages with jobs that actually involved theatre, sometimes as outreach directors, sometimes as teachers.[3]

From the Page to the Stage was my first job ever at Steppenwolf,

---

3. The very first acting class I signed up for in Chicago was with ensemble member Francis Guinan, who taught a scene study class in the basement of Halsted Street theatre. I predictably worked on a scene from *True West*.

and it did what I'd hope it would do: introduce me to the folks in the ensemble. And that led to other opportunities, including a couple more stints acting in S.T.C.'s educational outreach, a chance at directing my own educational outreach show, *The Effect of Gamma Rays on Man-in-the-Moon Marigolds*, and eventually an opportunity that would change my life forever, which I'll get to promptly. But before I do: a crisis of confidence.

* * *

By 1988, I'd had my fill of non-paying, or ultra low-paying, acting and directing gigs. I had been supporting myself primarily through crappy day jobs, such as slinging snickerdoodles at The Original Cookie Company on Chicago's Magnificent Mile, and working as a runner at the Chicago Board of Trade. When I came to Chicago, I had told myself I would give this theater thing five years, and if it wasn't working out, I'd switch to another tack, something less risky, more practical. Perhaps a business of some sort, or study to be an architect? I'd reached that five year marker and had a pretty good run. People knew me as an actor, but my real success came as a director, an arena in which I had managed a string of hit shows that culminated with a production of *The Normal Heart* at Next Theatre. Still, this was not enough for anyone, or any company, to give me steady work in the industry, or a shot at directing at any of Chicago's prestige, A-list theatres. I was barely making rent. So one day I woke up and decided the jig was up. I resigned from Lifeline, telling my colleagues I'd had enough, I was ready to leave the city and move in with my parents and figure out what I was going to do with the rest of my life.

Literally... as I was packing my bags, I got a call from Phyllis at Steppenwolf. She wanted to know if I would audition for a brand new play adaption of *The Grapes of Wrath*.

Now, I knew about this production. It had been getting a lot of buzz on the streets, first as a rumor, then as a real thing: Steppenwolf Theatre, known for its daring productions of American classics, was in discussions with the John Steinbeck Estate to do an epic, massive stage rendering of *The Grapes of Wrath*. Steppenwolf had also just broken ground for a brand new theatre. The company had continued its successes with plays and exporting stars to both coasts. *Grapes of Wrath* had never been adapted to the stage (except for a couple one-off productions), because Elaine Steinbeck, John Steinbeck's widow, feared it would never meet her, or the public's, expectations. But when she heard that Steppenwolf was interested, well, that was another matter. Frank Galati, then famous as a director in Chicago, and the most recent artist to join the Steppenwolf Ensemble, was to adapt and direct (it was his idea in the first place). The show would be epic—the biggest, most expensive S.T.C. production to date.

It didn't take me long to say yes to this audition. I realized I had, in my mind, left theater. But what the hell, the audition was an hour out of my life, tops, and as long as I was a winged seed blowing in the wind, why not see if that wind would take me in this direction?

I think part of the reason I was asked to audition—outside of my past association with the outreach program—was that by 1988 I had made a name for myself as a director. So maybe it was kind of cool to have me around? I don't know. Also, I had at that time a very distinct Okie kind of look, which one might say is a Steppenwolf kind of look, made famous by the likes of Terry Kinney, Gary Sinise, Tom Irwin and Randall Arney. A lean, gaunt face and frame (thank you subsistence living), hollowed out eyes and a loping gate. Years later, taking meetings in L.A., one producer, David Permut, took one look at me and blurted, "Well, you certainly *look* like a Steppenwolf guy." Auditioning for *Grapes*, the thought occurred to me I wasn't being considered for my talents as much as for my starving man silhouette. And sure enough, when I was offered a part—or parts—in the play, my roles were essentially Okie window-dressing (with an understudy assignment thrown in to sweeten the deal).

Getting cast in *The Grapes of Wrath* was a big deal, and I would have been an idiot to turn it down. At the very least, I was certain to get a couple good stories out of the deal. So I put my career change on hold, extended the lease of my hundred-dollar-a-month crappy apartment above the B.L.U.E.S. bar on Halsted and dove into rehearsals. This put a little strain on my relationship with my Lifeline cohorts, who were left scratching their heads about my sudden flip-flop on quitting the business. Sadly, they took it as a slight, and I was never able to keep up good relations with any of them afterwards. Which is sad to me. They gave me my first directing job—a collection of Harold Pinter One acts and blackout sketches we titled *Pinter Plays*—and a few decent acting roles. They taught me a lot about how a theatre is run and what it takes to bring in an audience, skills which would come in handy later on. They took a leap of faith with me, and for that, I will be forever grateful, because without Lifeline in my past, I'm quite certain I would have never made it into the folds of Steppenwolf.

✳ ✳ ✳

As I suspected, *The Grapes of Wrath* turned into one big adventure. And I ended up learning a hell of a lot from Frank Galati.

Up until this time in my career, I never really had a mentor, and certainly no one to teach me about directing and working with actors. There were programs and apprenticeships set up for this sort of thing—organizations like the Theatre Communications Group, who chose young directors and paired them up with companies like the Goodman. I applied many times to these, but never reached the interview stage.

The Grapes of Wrath on Broadway. This is a scene that depicts a flood at the end of the novel. I think I'm the guy center, back to the audience.

But here, *Grapes* created an instant opportunity, and I grabbed it. I could learn on the job. Not as an assistant to a director, but as an actor, who, let's face it, wasn't called on to do much of anything in this gigantic show but occasionally walk across the stage and blurt out a line here and there. I spent most of my time on the sidelines watching Frank, whom I knew I would never be able to match in style or intellectual acumen. Frank was a professor (at Northwestern University) as well as a director, and his genius was partly to inspire by way of his words. He had a knack of knowing what to say at exactly the right time, and expressing it in a way that inspired. As a director, Frank was sort of the opposite of the Steppenwolf actor, who was all spit and vinegar, instinct, bravura and assault. Frank would watch a scene that went off the rails—as they often did in *Grapes* rehearsals—and afterwards calmly articulate what we had all just experienced. Then he would gently set that scene back on the rails. He was, in a way, precisely what Steppenwolf needed at that time: context and definition for an acting style that had neither.

Frank really did not do much of anything while directing. He watched. And he was a captive audience. He threw the full weight of the production on the actors, who were grateful to have such an advocate, someone who would protect them from shame and catch them if they fell. Actors loved Frank, and Frank loved them back. I don't ever remember him being detached or morose. He was always encouraging and present. And universally respected.

I remember sitting near him one afternoon after a rehearsal on Broadway and overhearing a conversation with a colleague. Frank was contemplative and unusually quiet. The man he was with finally asked what was on his mind, and Frank said, after a long pause, "I'm trying to figure out how I'm going to tell the costume designer I don't like Ma Joad's hat."

He cared about people, and he knew the weight of his words— valuable lessons for any director attempting to corral a collective of widely divergent talents and personalities.

I also learned about how to nurture of a brand new piece of theater. Which was fortunate, because after *Grapes*, I would spend the rest of my career mostly creating new work.

* * *

Steppenwolf Theatre had always had an aura of mystery surrounding it. How did so many talented actors wind up in the same
small company that started in a church basement in Highland
Park, Illinois? The ensemble began with its founders, Gary Sinise,
Jeff Perry and Terry Kinney in 1974, but it wasn't until 1976 that
the ensemble came together. Jeff Perry and Terry Kinney had just
graduated from Illinois State where they recruited fellow actors
from that program: John Malkovich, Joan Allen, Laurie Metcalf,
Alan Wilder, Nancy Evans and H.E. Baccus. Not a bad group. The
company always claimed the secret ingredient was in the ensemble, the whole taking precedence over the individual, that made
the company what it was. This was true, that is clear. But how did
this group of people get there, and what exactly did they do to
create that level of ensemble? It's not as if other companies of actors
were trying to do the opposite. Ensemble had been the baseline
for any production since Stanislavsky. So what made Steppenwolf
different?

Grapes was my opportunity to find out. I was finally going to
get a glimpse behind the curtain, to learn the recipe for the secret
sauce. So I watched, and I took in all that I could. And what I
learned, especially from Gary, was that despite the company's pen-
chant for goofing off and irreverence towards anything status quo,
on stage the Steppenwolf actors were dead serious. Gary Sinise, as
Tom Joad, rehearsed as though his life depended on it, taking as
much time as he needed to discover the tiniest, genuine truth on
stage. Pauses between lines were sometimes so monumental that
anyone watching might think we were doing the five hour long
Kabuki version of Grapes.

Terry and Jeff were the same, searching for honesty in every line, every exchange, every moment. And if this was interrupted or disrupted, watch out, there would be hell to pay. Risks were taken. And encouraged. Any line reading was challenged time and again to discover, or rediscover, which was most authentic.

In this way, *The Grapes of Wrath* unfolded. We were given an extra two or three weeks of rehearsals, but even that wasn't enough to get where we needed to be by opening. The first preview—which was performed at the new The Royal George Theatre (now defunct) across the street from what would be the new Steppenwolf Theatre—was four hours long. People left at intermission, bored and confused. In this rendering of the play, Frank had added his own stamp of pretension (Frank was, after all, a tenured professor), crafting occasional surrealistic scenes that had nothing to do with plot progression or character development.

Over the next two weeks of previews, before we opened, Frank took a hatchet to the script, cutting sections, whole scenes and even supporting characters, till he reshaped the entire production. The cast was at first shellshocked, reeling from the wholesale changes, but eventually we pulled it together. We knew the show was in trouble. We worked overtime and followed Frank's lead. Ours was a leap of faith, but it was the only alternative in the multi-million dollar venture that Steppenwolf was betting would take the company to the next level.

And in the end it worked. By the time we opened in Chicago, the play had been winnowed down to a reasonable three hours, and scenes that were dead in the water before now blossomed. As a company, we could feel the show coming together and before long we knew we had a hit on our hands.

And I rode that massive production all the way from Chicago

to San Diego, where we had a run at La Jolla Playhouse, to London's National Theatre and then, finally, to Broadway, where the play ran for a little under six months after winning seven Tony Awards, including Best Production.

I took this picture outside the Cort Theatre on Broadway in 1990. Despite rave reviews and a Tony for Best Play, Grapes lasted only five months.

Before *Grapes*, I was 29 years old and flat broke. That play helped me get out of debt. I had been in Chicago, doing theater and working day jobs for over seven years. Now I was finally able to buy my first car.[4] *Grapes* got me my Actor's Equity card. And it was also a hell of a lot of fun. At the National Theatre in London, we were the toast of the town. The three or four weeks we spent there was like a paid vacation. And New York wasn't much different. The city was just recovering from the '70s and '80s Times Square crime and sex shop doldrums. The streets were getting cleaned

---

4. This was a no frills Toyota Tercel—really, no frills whatsoever, not even air conditioning

up, and money was being invested in a new, refurbished Broadway. I shared a modest apartment in midtown with Stage Manager Malcolm Ewen.[5] It was an exciting time. I got to know New York and navigate it like a pro (or at least an advanced beginner). And I could do this because I worked a mere four hours every evening. The rest of my time was taken up with exploring the city, playing softball in the Broadway Show League, and generally goofing off and causing trouble. The whole thing was all fun and games...

Till the stage fright kicked in.

* * *

Now I'm not really sure why or how it all began, but around the third month of the Broadway run, I started feeling increasingly apprehensive about going out on stage and getting my lines out. Maybe I fumbled a couple words one night—I don't know. But I remember somewhere around April feeling the terror that I might muff a line, or miss an entrance, or that maybe I would fall flat on my face, literally or metaphorically, and humiliate myself. In rehearsals there were moments during run-throughs when my mind would go completely blank. What if that happened in front of a paying audience? I reasoned that my fears might be the result of my bite-sized part in the play. I really was on the periphery. I played a Used Car Salesmen (one of five who came out, sang a song, and then promptly exited). I also played an Okie, and Another Okie (different from the first), and a character known simply as Man at Hooper Ranch, as well as Third Vigilante and Second Man

---

5. Malcom, a good friend, would come to stage manage scores of Steppenwolf productions over the years. He was diagnosed with cancer and succumbed to the disease in 2018, but not before he was invited into the ensemble as its first and only Production Stage Manager member.

in the Flood. Between all these characters I had… maybe ten lines? Any screw up would go under the microscope of those precious, nano-seconds when the spotlight shone on me. One error would be glaring, and far worse than if I'd had a more sizable role and the time and space to recover.

On stage, waiting for my cues, I remember getting tense and anxious. Forget artistry, would I even make sense of my lines? My goal was simply to get the words out. Performance after performance, this hell prison I had built for myself kept getting worse. This self-imposed pressure made performing a terror, not a joy. It became a nightmare I could not escape. I remember being on stage, saying my lines and hearing myself say them as I did. It was as if I was floating above myself, watching the facsimile of a human being expressing thoughts and forming words. Badly.

So. Five months into the Broadway run, when the phone rang and Randy Arney asked me if I would exit the show, get on a plane and come back to Chicago to direct a play, my answer was an unflinching, unequivocal and enthusiastic "Yes!" I had a solution to my problem. *The Grapes of Wrath* would be my first and last Actor's Equity job. I exited the cast and, as it turned out, never set foot on the stage again.

2

Yes And...

"If you come to a fork in the road, take it."

— Yogi Berra

SO THE OFFER TO PLAY DORN was, to say in the least, disruptive. Initially I was curious, then terrified. This would definitely take me outside my comfort zone, but then again I'm always up for a good adventure. And then I thought… there is that stage fright thing I left behind oh so many years ago. Do I run from that, or do I face it and confront it head on?

I looked at *Seagull*'s production calendar. First rehearsal was March 29th, opening scheduled for May 6th. The show would close on June 12th, with a possible two week extension. Well that ain't gonna happen. Or rather, maybe an extension would happen, but without me. Eleven weeks away from home was more than my limit.

I've worked out of town a lot over the years, but the longest I'm away is five weeks, tops, whenever I direct theater or opera. Recently it's been more opera than theatre and those rehearsals are generally shorter. *Seagull* would be longer than twice that, and during the school year, no less, when two parents, even for one kid, prove far better than one. And I can't say I wouldn't miss watching my son, Henry, turn seventeen. In another couple years he would be out of the house and on his own (theoretically anyway). Time away from him has always been at the top of my considerations when taking a job out of town.

I was ready to turn the offer down flat when Sue second-guessed me. Yeah, it would be a long time apart, but there were benefits. Sue, who is an actor, quite coincidentally and perhaps fortuitously, had been offered a movie that would be filming in Chicago about the same time. She and Henry could come and stay with me during her shooting days (which amounted to two one week stints). And besides, she reasoned, acting after so many years would be an interesting challenge. And it's not like I was doing anything in L.A. I couldn't do on off hours in Chicago. Writing is a job I can take anywhere. Why not at least consider the offer?

So I did. And I didn't exactly make a list of pros and cons, but I spent a lot of time mulling it over. I always thought the best writers were originally actors, or introverts unable or unwilling to come out of their shell. William Shakespeare, Moliere, Harold Pinter, David Mamet and Tom Stoppard were all actors before they became playwrights. Tarel McCraney and Dominique Morisseau and Tracy Letts are more recent examples. Anyway, my own experience was that I was never very good at writing plays or screenplays until I started thinking like an actor while writing them.

Another reason to take the job would be to watch another director at work. I'd known Yasen for years, but we didn't get a chance to work together till I directed him in my play *Lindiwe*. The production produced mixed results, but I liked working with

Yasen, who is from Bulgaria and was trained in theatre there. I thought I could learn something from him.

Also in the pro column: Chekhov! The master of ensemble playwriting, the actor's go-to master for dimensional, complex and endlessly interesting, challenging characters. Or so they say. As a director, I'd shied away from Chekhov when most of my theatre colleagues held him up as the messiah of modern theatre. He was the quintessential dramatist and renderer of the human condition. When directed properly, I was told, and with the right understanding, productions of his plays were unforgettable, transcendental, and life-transforming experiences.

The trouble is, these productions are few and far between. I, for one, had never seen one. The Chekhov productions I witnessed over the years were mostly dull, exposing the flaws in the plays rather than the virtues. Where others saw genius, I saw plots that circled around on themselves, employing characters that arrive exactly where they began. Over the course of my career, I had shied away from directing Chekhov. But this was acting. Sue was quick to point out that most actors would kill for a chance to act in *Seagull* at Steppenwolf. Perhaps if I acted in a production, I would understand the Chekhov mystique.

And there was another good reason for me to take the project. Since I moved to Los Angeles around 1998, I'd returned to Steppenwolf to direct and write, but these stints were few and far between. In the past decade, Steppenwolf had added more than a few members to its ranks, swelling to a membership of around 50. This would be an opportunity to reconnect with my artistic home and get to know some of the new Steppenwolfers.

* * *

Glenn Davis, one head of the two-headed artistic director team of Steppenwolf (along with Audrey Francis), called almost immediately after I had accepted the role. Over the phone, I could hear him grinning ear to ear.

"So I got the news," he said. "You're on board!"

"Yup."

"How long has it been since you were on the stage?"

"Thirty-two years, Glenn."

He laughed. "Wow, man. Thanks for doing this, you're gonna be awesome."

Then he said "Bye." Short call. And the thought occurred to me, maybe it was a joke after all. Maybe no one expected me to accept.

The next call, not five minutes later, came from Yasen, who was more sensitive but no less giddy.

"Well," he said in his easy Bulgarian accent, "I have all the confidence in the world, Eric, that you will be great."

Did he need confidence? Was I projecting apprehension? Already I could feel the jitters coming on, that weird hyper-sensitivity that only comes with being put on stage and under the microscope. The dormant actor side of me was waking up in a big way. Had I just made the biggest mistake of my career? How soon would it take till they fired me?

The next couple weeks I let the whole thing settle in, while secretly hoping that some big impossible-to-turn-down writing assignment might come through and give me a legitimate excuse to bow out. First rehearsal was still a couple months away. People backed out of plays all the time for more remunerative work. I could be one of those lucky bastards who "got a better job." In the meantime though, I thought, maybe I'll just start memorizing those lines. Because what are the chances that another job knocks this one off the block? Not great. And at the back of my brain, there was the memory of stage fright nagging me. The first order of business had to be learning those fucking lines. Confront the things that frighten you most and take them away one by one.

Yasen in rehearsal.

From that point on through to, well, the end of this entire escapade, memorization would become my obsession. And it wasn't just my *Grapes of Wrath* experience that was dictating this, but a memory from long ago. A short time after leaving *Grapes* and directing *The Secret Rapture*, things moved along pretty quickly for me at Steppenwolf. In quick succession, I was asked to be on the artistic staff, then I directed *The Song of Jacob Zulu* on Broadway, which became a big deal. The show featured the South

African singing group Ladysmith Black Mambazo and eventually was nominated for six Tony Awards. After that—this was 1993— Randy invited me into the ensemble, and I started directing at Steppenwolf on a pretty regular basis. One of my assignments was Tony Kushner's *Slavs!*, an erudite and sometimes comical look at the collapse of the Soviet Union. This was to be in S.T.C.'s smaller studio theatre, because it was a compact play that necessitated a modest production. The cast of characters featured four female and five male actors ages 10 to 90. At first I was very lucky with my cast. Martha Lavey, Amy Morton and Marianne Mayberry—all ensemble members—jumped on board, and I was able to wrangle Nate Davis, an excellent octogenarian actor (and also the son of film director Andrew Davis), as well as local veterans Jim Mohr, Bernie Landis, and Chicago regular Bill Norris. The last, older male actor to be cast was going to be a challenge, but there were candidates out there.

One of these was the father of a friend of mine who had a day job of an ad exec in a downtown Chicago firm. The man—let's call him Bob— was non-union, but that didn't matter. In Chicago, the acting pool was so vibrant and strong that it was often hard to tell the amateurs from the pros. Bob was a man who acted as a hobby, but his talents were nothing short of inspirational. He was a natural. Coming to theater at a late age, he tried out for a play on a dare, and won the part. After success in some small, below-the-radar productions, he started getting offers from directors at the more prominent Equity houses around the city.

But then tragedy struck, in a moment when the planets align in a way and seem to plot against an unsuspecting mortal. On the opening night of a new play at Northlight Theatre (still around!), waiting in the wings, on hearing his cue, Bob was instantly, inexplicably overcome with fear. And he stood there, stock still, refusing to go on. No amount of coaxing from stage management could budge him, while the actors on stage vamped and waited, helpless. Trapped and desperate, Bob chose the only reasonable option he thought available: he turned heel, bolted and left the theatre. He hoofed it across the parking lot, folded himself in his car and sped off. Never to return.

This event, a case study of an actor's nightmare, spread through the Chicago theater community like wildfire. Everyone talked about it, because it's a pretty damn good story. But also, I suppose, because it took away from the anxiety we all feel about failing miserably in public. Bob became a sacrificial lamb of sorts, the Tessie Hutchinson of our little colloquial lottery, the human sacrifice that allowed the rest of us to live our theatrical lives free from worry.

I knew Bob and his family, and I felt for them.

About the time I was casting *Slavs!* and beating the bushes for old farts to play Russian apparatchiks, I thought of Bob. I heard he had turned his full attention back to hustling ad accounts. But it had been a few years since that nightmare event at Northlight, and I wondered if he might be ready to give acting another shot. And doesn't everyone deserve a second chance? So I called Bob and asked if he would be interested in getting back on the boards? He didn't skip a beat: "Yes" came the quick reply. But could I send him the script? I sent him the play, and the very next day he called and accepted, telling me, "It would be an honor to be a part of this production."

I was elated. In that instant, I imagined Bob's performance. The

Chicago theater community would all come out to see him. They would be wowed by his performance and amazed at this improbable comeback: an actor kicks stage fright's ass. His humiliating exit from the theatre would be vindicated after a singularly triumphant performance in a brand new play by America's pre-eminent playwright.

The first day of rehearsal, Bob came prepared. He was completely off-book. Word perfect. There was not a trace of hesitation reciting his lines around the table. The cast was blown away—intimidated even—by his memorization prowess. A few of the older actors ragged on him for being such a Pollyanna. All the same, Bob's preparation cowed everyone else into working that much harder.

Then... a very strange thing happened. As rehearsals proceeded, Bob showed signs of a waning confidence. He would forget a word here or there and get knocked off track. Another day, an entire line would go out the window, and then a passage.The other actors, the staff and I watched in worried amazement as he proceeded to, day by day, forget every, single, word.

We reached the run-through stage and Bob continued to falter. By then it had become clear that this was not just some sort of cognitive degeneration (or dementia or whatever). We had seen Bob word perfect. He had conquered forgetfulness, he was free and clear. And then he lost it. He went down a rabbit hole of anxiety from which he seemed unable to return. During rehearsals, when he was not on stage, I would send him away with a production assistant to go over lines. But Bob didn't need time, he needed a psychiatrist.

Amy Morton as Bonfila Bezhukhovona Bonch-Bruevich, Bernie Landis as Babushka and Mariann Mayberry as Katherina Serafima Gleb in Steppenwolf Theatre Company's production of "Slavs!" by Tony Kushner. Directed by Eric Simonson, performances run through July 3, 1994 at the Steppenwolf Studio Theatre, 1650 N. Halsted Street, Chicago. For tickets call the Steppenwolf Box Office at (312) 335-1650. Copyright: Michael Brosilow.

A still from my production of Tony Kushner's Slavs! The late, great Bernie Landis (center) was not the "Bob" in my story. Bernie was Chicago theatre legend in his own right. Huge heart and endless invention.

Previews proved worse. Mariann Mayberry, who was Bob's main scene partner (she played a sado-masochistic punk rocker to Bob's aging bureaucrat) was understanding, but to a point. And eventually her patience ran out. She appealed to me privately: "We're dying up there" she told me. "It's just me and him on stage, and every look in his eyes is sheer terror." Forget about delivering a solid performance, she was just trying to get through the goddam scene without stopping the show dead in its tracks.

Then mid-previews, Tony Kushner came out from New York to check in on our progress. He had a stake in this show. It was only the second production of the play and the last stop before a New York premiere. I greeted Tony in the lobby before the performance and cooly chatted him up. I think at the time I was in denial, hoping against hope that he and the audience might appreciate Bob's long pauses between lines and rather slipshod delivery as a character choice meant to reflect the way some people actually talk.

No such luck.

That night, Bob's performance was once again disastrous. Whole sections went missing. Lines were ditched or brutally paraphrased. Bob's fear was palpable. Mariann was a trooper, but in the end, she was, unfortunately, forced to share the humiliation of an actor trying to salvage a scene doomed to fail.

After the performance I looked around for Tony—he was nowhere to be found. The house manager said something about seeing him slip into the administrative offices, just off the lobby. I went into the darkened room and searched, eventually finding him at my desk, shielded from the rest of the office by a couple cubicle partitions. His head was buried between his arms, hands clasped over his head, fingers laced together like a Chinese finger trap. I may be mistaken, but I think he was rocking back and forth in the manner of Dustin Hoffman's Rain Man. And in that instant, it was clear to me: Bob had to go.

I had never fired an actor before. It was inconceivable that I would ever do such a thing. It went against all my convictions of sticking with the team and never giving up. But there were other people I had to take into account— people like Mariann, helpless on stage, who needed an assist.

The next morning, I called Bob and asked him to meet me before rehearsal. He agreed without asking why, though I guessed he probably knew. Our meeting was uncomfortable, but short and to the point. I told him we needed to make a change. His line issues were getting in the way of presenting the play Tony had written, and that wasn't fair to him or anyone else. All the while I was talking, Bob nodded in agreement. This was a conversation that needed to happen, but it was clear he wanted to get it over with as soon as possible.

When I finished, Bob smiled and stood up. He shook my hand, and wished me luck. There was not a tinge of anger or animosity in his expression or manner. Mostly, he looked relieved. And I saw him for who he was: a 65 year old ad exec who picked up the gauntlet of a second chance and failed. Acting was not his world. Perhaps it never was. Perhaps, in the days when audiences marveled at his performances, he was merely executing a neat trick. Maybe his talent was not a talent at all, but an illusion.

Or maybe not. No one can take away the moments he gave audiences. His past, on-target performances were as real as the memories of them that people nurtured. Those existed. They were real. They *are* real.

Before he left, Bob asked me to pass along his regards to the rest of the cast and tell them he was sorry he couldn't say goodbye in person. Then he turned and left. Just like, I imagined, he had turned and left Northlight Theatre that night a few years before. And I never saw Bob again.

Stage fright once, shame on you. Stage fright twice... you never get the third shot, do you?

So. This was at the front of my brain as a prepared for *Seagull*. Were Bob's issues really, purely psychological? Who can say? All I knew was that I didn't want the same fate. I'd come close to disaster with *Grapes*, but steered clear it. What about now? Had I set myself up for failure? Maybe in the end, I would be forced to hang it all up—everything.

Just like Bob.

3

---·❦·---

An Actor Prepares

"Acting is everything but the words."

— Stella Adler

I STILL HAD A WHILE before first rehearsal. I recorded all the lines of the others characters in my scenes, and left pauses where I could recite my lines. I'd seen my wife do this on many occasions and thought "Great idea!" Dorn has… not a lot of scenes, certainly not as many as, say, Treplev and Nina, but more than I would have liked. And whenever I had a spare few minutes, or was on runs or walks, working out, putzing around the house, I would plug in my AirPods and run lines. It wasn't easy. In fact, the memorization was more difficult than I thought it would be, and I wondered if this was a skill professional actors develop over the years. I've seen older actors spew out veritable one person shows with ease. On the other hand, I've also witnessed my fair share of young actors struggling to pluck lines out of thin air.

And as I was memorizing, I became curious about the role I was about to play, and the world he inhabited. Dr. Dorn was clearly a version of Chekhov himself. So were two other characters in the play: the young aspiring writer/playwright Treplev, and the older, more cynical and established populist writer Trigorin. Put these three characters together, you get Chekhov.

Dorn is a doctor, as was Chekhov in real life, but unlike Chekhov, he is not an artist. He likes to hang *around* artists, and he has a philosophy of life that was a kind of mixture of nihilism and Epicureanism. He is a confirmed bachelor, a lady's man. He loves his freedom and, I guess, his many sexual exploits. And he has a joie de vivre that is refreshing, especially when set in sharp contrast to the collection of misanthropes that populate the story.

When I told my friend, actor Harry Lennix, that I was cast in this production, he said, after a delighted chuckle (by now I was getting used to this sort of reaction) "Wait a minute, is he—is that the guy who likes the play?"

"Yes" I said.

"I *like* that guy!" He said with enthusiasm.

I'm not sure why, but that stuck with me, and it became a big part of my understanding Dorn. Of all the people who watch Treplev's play (within the play) in the first act, Dorn is the only one who actually admits to liking it. And from that point on, despite his flaws, his narcissism, his cynical outlook on the world, he supports Treplev as an artist. Maybe this was Chekhov supporting himself, or seeing himself as the young, aspiring artist and knowing that the outside voice from an elder or mentor was so essential to the ego. I had certainly had my own struggles as a young artist and missed out on a mentor, or really anyone outside my parents, who encouraged me.

I began to do research. Because I remembered from my college days, and years of treading the boards in Chicago, that this is something actors sometimes do. There were other tasks, too, I remembered that I needed to do. Among them, write my character's biography. Also, write down what you say about yourself, and what other characters say about you. Invent a backstory and the facts of what happens just before and after all your character's entrances and exits. This is real basic stuff. Were these Stanislavsky exercises? I'm pretty sure they were. At least that's what I remembered. Or maybe they're just in the grand ethos of what all actors do and have done since Greek times. What was important was that I had the instinct, or impulse, to do these things. Does it all come back at once? Maybe not all of it, but the prep part—the getting the bike ready to take it for the ride part. It was all coming back pretty quickly.

I called Yasen and asked him for a recommendation of a Chekhov biography because I realized, in my long avoidance of all things Chekhov, that I knew practically nothing about the man. The book he suggested, though, was out of print and used copies were nowhere to be found. So I scoured Amazon for other bios and decided my best option was a book entitled *Anton Chekhov: A Life* by Donald Rayfield. Later, when I told Yasen I had instead read this biography, his brow furrowed into a knot of sympathy and guilt. He knew the book, had read it, and apologized for its tedious, workaday account of Chekhov's life.

And that it was. The book is literally a listing of everything Chekhov did, where he went, what he wrote, every, single, day of his life. And this begs the question: How did they know? I mean, this was turn of the last century, when there was no GPS, no cell phone logs, no e-mail trails. Yet this biographer was able to collect a day to day account of, not only where Chekhov was in the world, but what he did and wrote, what he said to others and what his friends and family were doing at the same time. I guess people just wrote a fucking hell of a lot in diaries and letters to one another. A lot more than they maybe do now. Still, it's an impressive accomplishment to put it all together, as Rayfield did. Albeit a tedious task, but for me, indispensable. The mosaic of day to day activities and writings gave me a worm's eye account of an ambitious man caught in the web of an oppressive society, and someone determined to express the truths of the human condition. It also gave detailed accounts of Chekhov as a bit of a slutty whore who resisted the pressure to marry and settle down. A man who, frankly, copulated his way through life and enjoyed it immensely—all the while battling chronic tuberculosis and churning out masterpieces. It was this volatile mix of embracing life in the face of death, I think, that resulted in his existential angst and perennial ennui. Through this exhaustive chronicle, I was able to confirm that Chekhov drew inspiration directly from his own experience. Playing literary detective, I also found many details of his life, and the people he met, woven into *Seagull*'s story and characters. For example, I got a clearer picture of the play's setting. The estate at which the characters congregate was not unlike country houses Chekhov visited throughout his life, and probably a lot like the one he built for himself, which he called Melikhovo.

Another example: right before writing *Seagull*, Chekhov was involved with a woman infatuated with him to the extent that she gave him a medallion with an inscription that read "If you want my life, take it." The exact same words used in the medallion that Nina gives Trigorin.[6]

---

6. Yasen confirmed the extent to which Chekhov infused his plays with his life.

Many more examples of the real world crashing in to Chekhov's imagined world exist. And it struck me how little has changed in the art of playwriting, or maybe writing in general. Most playwrights will tell you they are not just one character in their story, but a little bit of all the characters.

Dorn is a doctor. So was Chekhov. Dorn is a philosopher. Chekhov was one as well. He gave these parts of himself to Dorn. And also his encouragement of Treplev, whom he treats like a son. Dorn thinks about plays, theater, and the people who create these things. He has strong opinions about art and artists, but he is not one himself. Maybe he wishes he was. Instead, he lives life vicariously through the bohemians he meets and mingles with. He observes them and, at least in Treplev's case, takes them under his wing, nurtures them and plays the wise sage who points them in the right direction.

Dorn is an observer. One of the things I thought I'd try is find places in the play Dorn might have become the writer Chekhov was. Maybe Dorn is the version of Chekhov if he had not had the courage to become a writer. I imagined Dorn as Chekhov the doctor, *before* he became a writer, taking in the foibles, inconsistencies, tragedies, comedies, and the absurdities of human nature, so that he could one day write this story—*Seagull*—later in life.

Another thing I did before rehearsals began, and while I was dutifully going over lines (always the memorization) was read Chekhov's short stories and other plays. I also read as many translations of *Seagull* I could get my hands on. The short stories were interesting, but not as compelling as the plays. At least not for

---

The playwright allowed this actual medallion to be the prop used in the premiere production in 1896.

me, and I have to believe most of today's attention deficit audiences would feel the same. The zenith of the golden age of Russian literature—Tolstoy, Dostoyevsky, Turgenev—came at the time that Chekhov was writing. But with these authors, rich characters are woven into intricate and equally rich plots, sweeping the reader up in the world of the stories. Chekhov, who was considered an outlier in his day, is more interested in capturing a moment in time than weaving a good yarn. And this got me thinking of the things Dorn says about the fictional Treplev's writing, that "he creates impressions and nothing more, and you can't go far on impressions alone." This sounds an awful lot like Chekhov describing his own short stories. And I can't help thinking he used Dorn as a conduit to express his own frustrations with his critics, as he, like Treplev, strove to create something brand new. I think Chekhov knew his writing was innovative for its time, and that he was bucking up against the plot driven mega-novels of his day. Despite the success he had while he was alive, he was forever taking on the barbs of vicious critics and jealous literary rivals, who found his writing strange and tedious. *Seagull*, by way of Dorn, might have been a stealth way to defend his ideas about his own work.[7]

* * *

March 29th, our first rehearsal, was fast approaching and there was still no sign of a better alternative job on the horizon. I guess I was going to be going back on the boards after all—the reality of this started to sink in. To make matters worse, after two months of memorization, I was still having trouble getting my lines to stick.

---

7. And it needed defending. The premiere of *Seagull* was a disaster, with many of Chekhov's sharpest critics in attendance booing and hissing the performance as it was being played out.

Shouldn't I be able to recite them backwards and forwards by now? Had my 61-year-old, swiss-cheese brain devolved to zero memory recall?

And this always lead to that perennial, nagging question: Will I suffer the same fate as Bob?

I comforted myself with thoughts that once I was on my feet, muscle memory would kick in. Memorizing lines out of thin air was one thing. Acting and doing, attaching action to words—that would fix it.

Right?

* * *

Just because I was acting, didn't mean I left my day job. Over the past decade or so, I've made my living primarily as a writer. And my way of sustaining that living has been to juggle as many jobs, and prospective jobs, as possible. I joke to my friends that I'm a plate spinner, the guy who appeared regularly on *The Ed Sullivan Show* spinning plates on long sticks and then balancing them way up in the air, all at the same time. That guy would stand in front of a table and balance one, two, now five plates on top of skinny poles while flipping another five discs on the table, whirling them like dervishes. The feat required going back and forth between plates, regenerating them like tops whenever they began to flail and threaten to topple over, smashing to the ground. It was a nail-biting and daring feat. And also a perfect metaphor for anyone trying to maintain the freelance artist existence.

Back when I was in my 20s, the day jobs that supported me were menial, mostly waiting tables, sometimes moving furniture—whatever paid the rent. And I worked as many jobs as I could handle. And as many theatre gigs—paying or otherwise:

generating new projects, taking classes, auditioning, directing, acting. I did late-night shows, off-loop shows, off-off-loop shows, I staged readings of new plays. If I wasn't busy, I wasn't learning. I concluded that the "way of the artist" was not so much discipline and consistency in one's craft, as taking as many gigs as possible in the hopes that one day the gigs would outnumber the jobs. And that happened, eventually. Before long I was able to support myself with my art, but not without pooling the funds from several different projects at the same time.

This practice turned into habit, and 35 years later, I'm still spinning plates. I have a white erase board in my home office with a rotating list of no less than 20 projects in various stages of development. Over the course of weeks, months and sometimes years, projects go off the board, new ones come on. Some go through a natural process of development and on to fruition, and a finished product. These are the lucky ducks that get seen by an audience! Others are abruptly aborted or abandoned when all options for survival have been exhausted. Some are high paying gigs, others mere pipe dreams in search of an angel. Regardless of their financial worth or age, all of these projects comfort me. Mostly. Sometimes, especially in the case of the orphaned projects, they haunt and sadden me. Plays or television shows I developed that never saw the light of day still live with me. Sometimes I catch myself thinking about a certain play or show. The project had failed and existed only in my head, but by way of my imagination, I convinced myself it actually made it into the real world. The characters I create, and the scenarios I put them in are that real to me. In any event, these projects are my life's blood, and my white erase board—my list of hopes and dreams—will always be with me as long as I continue to create. Which will hopefully be for years to come.

Taking on *Seagull* would put many of these projects (my babies) on hold. I would have some hours outside of rehearsal, but not that many. I had been away from acting a while, but not long enough to forget that the demands it places on a person—physically, emotionally and practically—are extensive. When you're not in rehearsal, you're thinking about your character. It's a 24/7 assignment that demands constant attention and won't let go.

Seagull would be my primary focus, everything else would have to wait. So I made a few calls and warned collaborators on other projects I would be out of touch for a while.

And then, on March 28th, I said goodbye to Sue and Henry, and our little mutt, Pippen, and the comfort of my home and my man-cave office in Glendale, California, and I set off for Chicago.

4

First Day of School

"Acting is easy... once you get it."

— Byrne Piven

STEPPENWOLF'S DECISION to open its new theater with a production of a Chekhov classic was no accident. The company had made a reputation for itself as an ensemble theatre with a capital "E", and Chekhov was famous for writing plays for ensembles. The notion that the whole was greater than the sum of its parts, that marquee players meant less than whatever happened on stage in between the rank and file was at the heart of the company's core philosophy. All actors are born equal. Though Steppenwolf had made its name with productions of new and modern plays like *Balm in Gilead*, *True West*, *The Song of Jacob Zulu* and *August: Osage County*, the company always reliably, if infrequently, went back the well of Anton Chekhov, the father of ensemble acting, the guru of artistic equal opportunity. *Three Sisters*, *Uncle Vanya*, and *The Cherry Orchard* all had productions at Steppenwolf. Of the four big Chekhov plays, only *Seagull* had never been tried. Which is ironic, because the play is about, at least in part, theater, art, and artists.

In March, 2022, Steppenwolf was just about to unveil its new theater complex: an in-the-round 400 seat facility, situated just to the south of its more traditional 500 seat proscenium. The new space featured the aptly dubbed Ensemble Theatre, but also included a few new rooms for meeting and educational outreach purposes. There was also a tiny library and a smallish new bar in a roomy lobby. Our "black box" space in the old theatre complex was transformed into rehearsal rooms and there were lots of other cosmetic improvements. The whole thing had a price tag of over 54 million dollars.

When I entered the rehearsal room the first day, I had been in Chicago less than 24 hours. I was still a bit wobbly. And I had been distracted with settling into my apartment on the near north side. Nice digs, for sure—a corporate rental with floor to ceiling glass walls that, in a trick M. C. Escher could have appreciated, showed off three sides of Chicago. But I suffer from insomnia whenever I'm away from home, and the night before was a rough one. So the morning of March 29th—first rehearsal—I was feeling a little out of sorts.

As is usual on day one, there were many, *many* people. The place was lousy with folks. Some I knew, others I knew by sight but had never met, and still others I'd never even seen before. The room buzzed with anticipation. I managed to get in a few brief hellos to folks I knew, not saying much, nervous I'd reveal my secret terror over the impending read-through. I was glad to see Jeff Perry. A familiar face. And what a face—moon-shaped with large, saucer eyes and an open mouth that denies any hint of guile. Behind that friendly mask is a focus that knows what it wants. And for a lifetime, that want has been to make sure Steppenwolf—the theatre he had co-founded—would thrive and survive. Jeff was cast as Sorin, the aged and ailing Uncle to Treplev, and perennial gadfly to Dorn. We had a couple scenes together.

Jeff Perry as Sorin.

I had met newish ensemble members Caroline Neff, playing Nina, and Namir Smallwood, Treplev, at Steppenwolf functions before, but our conversations never went beyond small talk. Two other Steppenwolfers, Karen Rodriguez and Sandra Marquez, were playing Masha and Polina respectively. I had only seen them on stage but had never had a conversation with either. Getting to work with them was one of the reasons I took on this assignment. How odd it was that I am in the same theatre company as these people I hardly knew. The cast was rounded out with Jon Hudson Odom playing the school teacher Medvedenko, Joey Slotnik as Trigorin,

Lusia Strus playing Arcadina, and Elijah Newman as Yakov. Keith Kupferer, whom I had directed years before in my play *Carter's Way*, is one of those rare actors who can play rough-hewn, proletariat characters believably, and this was no exception—he was aptly cast as the country house manager Shamrayev. Joey Slotnik and I knew each other through friends and work. So all in all, a pretty familiar group.

Yasen was at the far end of the rehearsal hall glad-handing, hugging, and gesticulating wildly to all he encountered. He was clearly excited. His exuberance made me nervous, and I revisited the fear that, yes, he had cast me, but alas, he'd never seen me act. Hardly anyone in the room had. In fact, the only person was Jeff Perry. We were in *The Grapes of Wrath* together, years before, when he played Noah Joad and I played Third Okie From The Right. Did he remember me in that production? And even if he remembered me, would he have been able to ascertain whether I had any talent?

I wandered over to a wall where costume renderings had been posted, crafted by the excellent Ana Kuzmanic, a tall, willowy, and bespectacled designer born in the former Yugoslavia. Among the dozen or so watercolors, there were two renderings of Dorn. Both had the character dressed in leather and high waisted khakis: Indiana Jones. He wore a fedora and a vest, and looked more adventurist than general practitioner. All that was missing was the whip and an elephant gun. A month previous, Yasen and I had discussed costumes and hair.

"What about Dorn's hair?" I asked. I should mention I'm bald—well, for all intents and purposes. I had nurtured a skull stubble for years, recently waved the white flag and shaved my head completely. But I had this shallow idea that Dorn, as the confirmed bachelor of the group, should have a full head of wavy, sexy hair. And though I had some trepidation about applying something phony to my persona, I was looking forward to anything that would make me look like someone else. I liked the idea of a disguise. My argument to Yasen, though—at least the one I put forward—was that Dorn should be a free spirit, unencumbered by relationships and family ties. Yasen told me we were thinking in the same brain channel: Dorn as kind of an adventurist doctor, traveling the globe, cavorting with bohemians in between stints at home treating patients.

"Yeah so, the hair!" Yasen shot back, "I think of him as the Sean Connery version of Indiana Jones."

"Oh. So… no hair?" I asked.

"Yes! No hair. Like you. Bald! Some people have great skulls for no hair. I am not like that." (Yasen had little hair.) "I hate the shape of my head, but you. Your skull is a great shape for being bald! I love it!"

Was he shitting me? Trying to get me to do something for some other reason? As a director, I know these ruses, conjuring up a reason that sends the actor off the scent of a request that cannot possibly be granted.

And I guessed right. After some prodding Yasen admitted that Joey Slotnik, cast as Trigorin, had already been promised a wig and the company had no room in the budget for a second one. Wigs, by the way—good ones anyway—are notoriously expensive. They can run into the thousands.

I turned from the renderings back to the room, which was now twice as crowded and filled with even more chatter. And suddenly the whole scheme seemed absolutely absurd to me. Why was

I here? Did I know what I was doing? I'm a fraud.

Before I let these dark thoughts spin out of control, the room was called to order and quietened down, and we were all encouraged to come together for our first rehearsal.

* * *

To my relief, the first read through went well enough. I was nervous, but not cripplingly so, and it helped to learn others were nervous as well. I could tell by the missteps, the stops and starts. Some were better than others. I've always been horrible at cold readings, or rather, public readings. It's another reason I'd left acting. Auditions were hell for me. I would be given a scene to read cold, on the spot, and I'd invariably stumble over words and flub lines. Clean reading was a talent I never had, going all the way back to grade school. I remember my fourth grade teacher, Miss Bieder, calling on students to read out loud, and I would pray she wouldn't call on me. Did I suffer from dyslexia? I was never diagnosed, but I sure as hell had all the symptoms. And still do to this day. I was forever in the third reading group throughout most of grade school—a shameful public humiliation if ever there was one, and on display for all the other kids to see. As an adult, every script I read I experience in real time, the way a first audience might, because that's how fast (or slowly) I read. This gives me the time necessary to visualize a production, and by the end of the play, I have pretty much formed an idea about what I want to do, how it should look, sound and feel.

Still, with *Seagull*, I was prepared. This reading wasn't cold, at least for me, because I'd been going over these lines for two months straight. And that took some of the fear out of the experience. While reading Dorn for the first time, I realized I'd made

some pretty significant choices about the character. I knew Dorn a
womanizer, but this part of him sort of came out as sort of creepy.
I heard myself saying lines that made him more seductive than I'd
imagined in my head.

I keep a notebook (clearly). This is from the first day of rehearsal: my "Hi, my name is:" sticker and a sketch of a mask. In the spring of 2022, we were still required to wear masks while in rehearsal, and Covid-19 tests were administered regularly. The phonetic spelling of Zarechnaya, Nina's last name, was a word I could never pronounce to Yasen's satisfaction.

My latching on to Dorn's enthusiasm over Treplev's play came
out as a bit overzealous too. Again, the voice inside my head was
very different from the one the left my mouth. I'd made a choice
that Dorn was a fan of Treplev, but this guy—the guy at the table
read—was downright hysterical. He didn't just like the play, he

really, really *liked the play!* That particular line was met with a few chuckles mixed with genuine fear. Too far? Guess I'd find out. Reading other translations of Seagull, it was clear Chekhov meant to convey that Dorn liked the play, but the verdict was out as to what extent. There were definitely more subdued—even ironic—interpretations.

Another takeaway from the first read: our cast was kick-ass. Not only were they good individually, but it felt like we were all acting in the same play, in the same style, which can be a problem with Chekhov. If some actors were more inclined to lean into the "classical" approach to Chekhov, I think that might have been a problem. But no one was. We were all pretty much acting in a believably naturalistic, contemporary style. Every line, every interaction, was approached as accessible and genuine. So maybe it was luck, or a conscious part on Yasen's part, but the cast had the real potential, I felt, to congeal into a unified group.

The reading finished and, as is always the case, there was polite applause followed by a collective look to the writer/adapter, Yasen, who, switching over to his director's hat, offered up a few props, "Good job, I'm excited," and then finally, "Let's take a break."

And my first instinct was to retreat into myself, because no matter what I thought about how I did, or how excited I was about the prospects for the show, who knows what everyone else thought. So many conversations and comments from entering the rehearsal hall to the start of the read were jabs about me not acting in a while. "So they pulled you out of retirement, eh?" "When I heard you were in the cast I had to think, has he ever even acted before?" That sort of thing.

During the break I pretended to check my phone, which turned into *actually* checking my phone. I sneaked into an adjacent room (an enormous, empty hall which would soon become our rehearsal space) and made some business calls. In the middle of one of them, Yasen passed by, saw me and stopped. He gave me a big smile and a thumbs up. I waved, and after he disappeared, exhaled relief.

Little did I know, that would be the last bit of encouragement I would get for weeks.

5

---·⟨∞⟩·---

The Rear View Mirror

*"And Lot's wife, of course, was told not to look back
where all those people and their homes had been. But she
did look back, and I love her for that, because it was so
human. So she was turned into a pillar of salt. So it goes."*
— Kurt Vonnegut, *Slaughterhouse-Five*

IT HAD BEEN A WHILE since I'd spent any length of time
in Chicago. I lived there for 15 years, from 1983 to 1998. I left when
I decided I'd had enough of the Chicago winters. And the traffic
as well. It strikes others as odd whenever I say I think the traffic in
Chicago is actually worse than in L.A., but I really believe that. In
L.A., one can control traffic according to the time of day. I schedule
all my meetings mid-day to avoid rush hours. And yes, I realize
I am lucky I have a job that allows me to schedule my driving
times, but there you have it. I came to L.A. for the business—as
a freelance writer and director—and that business is perfect for
traffic. In Chicago, or at least the parts I lived in (Lincoln Park,
Wrigleyville, Lakeview), I would more often than not get stuck in
surface street traffic jams, bumper to bumper, thwarted by un-ti-

med lights and suburban tourists. It was worst on weekends, and summers on any day were downright horrible, with all the festivals and airshows. I remember sitting in my car one morning, in slow-and-go traffic on Clybourn, on my way from my condo on Wrightwood to Steppenwolf on North and Halsted (about a ten block trip), and watching an 80 year old man on the sidewalk pass me on foot several times as I stopped and waited, stopped and waited. Traffic in Chicago drove me nuts. And truthfully, it was one of the reasons I left.

Since I moved to L.A., I had come back to Chicago now and then to direct plays, but these stints lasted all of five weeks, during which any available time I had outside of rehearsal was devoted to future projects. When I was acting in *The Grapes of Wrath* in New York, it felt like a little vacation. Not to say that acting doesn't require talent, hard work and commitment, but the director and writer of any project takes on the weight and responsibility required to deliver a hit show. The onus is really on them, captain of the ship, the one with the overall vision.

In *Seagull*, I was looking forward to that not-being-in-charge part of the production. If this was anything like acting in *Grapes*, I would get some time off and the chance to treat this stint like a busman's holiday, maybe reacquaint myself with a city I once called home.

Looking back, my run in Chicago theatre, at the very start of my career, was a series of missteps, frustrations and eventually, a few lucky breaks. Occasionally, for fun, I sometimes trace the history of my life, or career, by tracking it back from one decision to the next. If I had something that worked for me artistically—a hit show or whatever—how did that happen? I need to find the source.

Was it an accident, or did it begin with one very prescient choice I made at a single moment in time? Mostly, I'm of the mind that whatever success I've had has been a combination of 25% smarts and 75% being in the right place at the right time. On one day off from *Seagull* rehearsal, I decided to take a tour of some of my old haunts and this sent me up to Wrigleyville, where I shared a basement apartment with my old pal Evan Gore. Evan and I knew one another from Madison, where I did a little improv right after college. We were both in a company called The Ark Repertory Theatre, which was not actually a theatre (let alone one that had a repertory). It was more a bunch of young punks playing for laughs on a tiny stage in a bar (more on this later). Most of us in the company eventually ended up in Chicago, and Evan and I became roommates. And we developed a very good talent for finding dirt cheap apartments. One of these was on the corner of Waveland and Halsted. A dingy two bedroom, with a bath (but no shower) in the basement of a five story complex. The place had little light, few comforts and wall to wall carpeting we called the Rug of a Thousand Dusts. But hey, who cared at 100 bucks a month .

It was around this time I was holding down several jobs, some theatre related, others not. I was doing my plate-spinning, and making friends, and dating actresses and going out to clubs and seeing lots and lots of theatre. Aside from the poverty, I look back on this as a pretty good time in my life.

One of the first people I became pals with in Chicago was Larry Sloan, whom I met through the folks at Lifeline (they all knew each other from Northwestern University). Larry was a tall, fresh kid just out of college, but his wisdom and caustic sense of humor belied his boyish looks. He was an old man trapped in a young man's body. When I first met Larry, he had made fast work getting known by all the right people in the Chicago theatre scene. Larry had an internship at the Goodman Theatre, where he impressed then Artistic Director Greg Mosher enough to promote him to the artistic staff as some sort of associate. He was making a name for himself as a talent to watch. But thinking back, I wonder what that talent was. Larry wasn't a director exactly and definitely not an actor or writer. It turned out what he was good at was producing and artistic directing. In particular, at Remains Theatre, but that was much later. At the time we were hanging out with each other, one thing was certain—Larry had his wits about him and he was good for advice. He gave me tons of insight on how to navigate the tricky, incestuous waters of Chicago Theatre. Larry introduced me to Brian Finn, who was the co-artistic director of a small but promising theatre called Next. Brian and his artistic director partner, Harriet Spizziri, a mercurial middle-aged woman with a heart of gold, saw something in me and cast me in two of their shows (one of which was the aforementioned *Blue Champagne*). At the same time, I was making a name for myself as a director, and when, in 1987, Next got the rights to produce the Chicago premiere of *The Normal Heart*, Harriet called on me to direct. This was a big break and led to everything else that was good for my career.

But before any of that happened, Larry introduced me to another person who would become a significant presence in my life: a young playwright named Scott McPherson.

Scott was an actor when I met him after his performance of a new play called *Butler County* by Dean Corwin at Victory Gardens Theatre. Watching him on stage, I was instantly struck by his charisma. You couldn't keep your eyes off him, and when he left the stage you felt the play had disappeared altogether. Scott had a lean, lanky build, and a thick coif of golden brown hair that took off in a wave across his forehead, then down over the side of his face. He had a bit of a southern twang that came, I suppose, from his upbringing in the lower class parts of Columbus, Ohio.

Scott (left) and Larry (right), after a photo taken by Suzanne Plunkett.

Larry, Scott, and I went out for drinks after the show at an old theatre haunt down the street called John Barleycorn's (now defunct), and I was immediately struck by his quick wit and easy banter. Everything he said was a set up for a punchline, or the punchline itself. I took an instant liking to him. I remember he wore a black and white *Nancy and Sluggo* t-shirt, which I found amusing. *Nancy and Sluggo*, for those not in the know, was the epitome of the worst, most remedial syndicated comic strip of its day. It took a second to read and was never funny, just plain dumb. Scott's t-shirt was a perfect insight to his ironic sense of humor.

The next time I saw Scott was by accident. I spotted him on the street, on his way home from the gym and we walked together for a while. The conversation was more like we knew one another longer than we had, and Scott went right to the familiar. He confessed he was struggling with a recent sexual encounter. A couple days before, he had been following a guy home from the gym—not intentionally but coincidentally. But the guy assumed otherwise and invited him up to his apartment, where they had sex, after which the guy abruptly told him to leave. Scott had never done anything like that before, apparently, and wondered if he should have. It didn't seem like he was going through any serious moral dilemma, more carrying on a conversation with a mere stranger about the details of an accidental hook-up. At a loss for a comeback, I promptly switched up the conversation to theatre—my favorite subject. I was at that time acting in a show at Lifeline and having a pretty rough time of it. I told him I was looking for something I could direct. Scott told me he had a play he wanted to get produced—his first—and wondered if I wouldn't mind taking a look at it.

That play turned out to be *Till the Fat Lady Sings*, a dark comedy about a young kid traumatized by his grandmother's death and his mother's unwillingness to mourn properly and soulfully. I remember reading the script and laughing so hard I cried. Scott was a very funny man, and an even funnier writer. And the play had a lot of heart, and pathos too. It was based a little on his relationship with his mom and a death in their family. It was filled with vivid, eccentric characters that elicited nervous laughs and heartfelt tears in equal measure. It was also a bit uneven and unwieldy, a clear test run for Scott's seminal, more sophisticated play *Marvin's Room*, which he would write later.

Directing Coriolanus at Next Theatre in Evanston in 1989. We made it work on practically zero funds. Working from nothing is how I learned to do theatre and to this day, whenever I direct a show, I worry constantly about budget. Left to right: Sarah DiVencentis, Deanna Dunagan, me, and Steve Pickering.

I loved this play. I understood it, I connected with it and, perhaps more importantly, it was new and fresh and had a sensibility that spoke to the times and my generation. And also, I had the playwright's permission to direct it. So I pitched the play to Lifeline. Remember, this was my plan all along, to act, and then, through relationships, gain the confidence of others who might let me direct. I had already had a little success with *Pinter Plays*. *Fat Lady* would be my second directing assignment and first try at an original work. I can't remember if there was any resistance from the Lifeline folks, but it was approved and slated for the next season pretty quickly. We had a terrific non-equity cast led by Lee Guthrie, who became close with Scott (and was, by the way, the inspiration for the role of Lee in *Marvin's Room*). The play was definitely flawed and the production probably brought out the weaknesses in the writing, but audiences loved it, and so did critics. Lifeline added performances and the show became a minor hit.

Till the Fat Lady Sings was also responsible for my next directing gig, *Waiting for Godot* at Bailiwick Theatre (now defunct). "No one hires you as a director till they've seen your work". It took me over four years, but I finally beat the Catch 22. *Waiting for Godot* also did well with critics and audiences, and that gave Harriet Spizziri the confidence to hire me to direct *The Normal Heart*. See what I'm doing here? I'm following the path back to where it all started, and for me it started with acting, which led me to Lifeline, which introduced me to Larry, who introduced me to Scott, who entrusted me with his play.

But there's more, at least where Scott is concerned.

After *Till the Fat Lady Sings*, I cast Scott in *The Normal Heart*, where he played Tommy, the sympathetic Southerner and neophyte activist. That production had a long life, and we stayed in close contact and began, as young folks do, plotting out our dreams for the future. I remember one afternoon over lunch at the Belden Deli (now defunct), Scott suggested we work on film projects, not just theatre projects.

"As long as we're broke and knocking our heads against a wall," I remember him saying, "we might as well knock them against a big wall."

I was all for that. I'd always had film in my sights, I knew it would be somewhere in my future, and I wasn't interested in living the proverbial life of the starving artist. So we came up with a few projects. Scott had tons of ideas for films, but he also threw in a few plays too. Why the hell not? We reasoned we should work on theatre, where we stood a fighting chance, while we developed the films we were certainly going to produce in years to come. One of his ideas was something he called *Marvin's Room*. Like *Fat Lady* it was based on real life, his own life. It was about a mother and her two children who are compelled to help an estranged older sister/ aunt, diagnosed with a terminal disease. The sister, Bessie, is the good daughter of the family and has devoted her life to caring for her aging father. Her sister, Lee, is a selfish ne'er-do-well black sheep, but she finds it in her heart to help Bessie in her time of need. The play, Scott told me, was an allegory for the AIDS crisis and how so many gay men were feeling isolated from the rest of the public and, as a result, called upon one another for support and help. Both of us were just coming off *The Normal Heart* and AIDS was fresh on our minds. In fact, working on that play, it was hard to think about anything but. The neglect that was going on at the time, the sheer cruelty and negligence from the government and the public, was infuriating. Scott's play would be a way to put the crisis forward in a way that everyone—not just the gay community and their allies but all Americans—could understand. As Scott told me the story, I could see it play out in my mind. Everything about it was crystal clear—the characters, the way it looked. I was immediately, emotionally drawn in, and I knew in that instant that this had to be our next project.

Pre Marvin's Room, Scott McPherson at the Chicago Historical Society. I got him this job, where I photographed artifacts. Scott packed items for museum storage. These photos were taken on Halloween, when we all dressed as our favorite artifact. Scott was a scissors.

From that day forward, Scott made *Marvin's Room* his focus. Every few days he would drop by my basement apartment and we would sit on the floor across from one another, take on different parts and read each new scene. Then we would talk about it. Usually it was me just encouraging Scott to "Keep going!" Then

Scott would leave and write some more, and we'd repeat the cycle. Till he finished the play. And when it was finished, I remember both of us sitting on the floor, atop that old dingy wall to wall, and taking a deep breath. It was a good play. We both knew it. Far superior to *Till the Fat Lady Sings*. Cleaner, better structured with a more sophisticated emotional reach that resonated beyond the surge of the story. Maybe, we thought, this was as good as any play anywhere.

I arranged for a reading at Steppenwolf, where, by then, I had been working pretty steadily on outreach programs. Ensemble member Rondi Reed helped me reserve the rehearsal room on the second floor of the theatre. She also agreed to read the role of Bessie. Lee Guthrie would take on the part Scott wrote for her (Lee). I leaned on a few friends to fill in the rest of the roles, and one night we all gathered to sit down and read the play. And that's when I knew for sure that Scott and I had something special. As the actors read the last scene, I looked around and there wasn't a dry eye. The play was working. It was moving people and sending a message. It ignited both the head and the heart—the ultimate goal of any good piece of theatre.

End of play, the actors gave Scott a round of applause and the room opened up to ebullient chatter. A lot of compliments came Scott's way as well as questions about next steps. But my sights were set on Rondi. I wondered, would she feel compelled to recommend the script to Steppenwolf? I watched as she collected her things and made a bee-line for the door. She apologized—she needed to be somewhere. There were still tears in her eyes when she thanked me for inviting her, and then added: "Needs work." And she was gone.

Those weren't the words I was looking for.

The next day I called Rondi to follow up. Despite the brush off, I was still convinced I could change her mind. No such luck. Rondi just didn't think the play was ready. Or maybe this just wasn't her kind of play. Whatever the reason, that put an abrupt end to my dreams of getting *Marvin's Room* produced at Steppenwolf. We would have to go somewhere else.

It was at this time, right after the Steppenwolf reading, that Scott let loose with a bombshell: *Marvin's Room* wasn't just an allegory about the AIDS crisis. Scott actually had AIDS—he was H.I.V. positive. The news hit me like a thunderbolt. Despite the fact that we were in the middle of the AIDS epidemic, at the time I did not know anyone who actually had contracted the disease. That Scott had written this play as an allegory of the AIDS crisis must have blinded me to the fact that he himself might be afflicted. A case of the Purloined Letter, the opposite of Occam's razor: Scott can't possibly have AIDS—he's the author of a made up *story* about AIDS.

This was 1988, when there was no cure for the disease. Getting diagnosed was a virtual death sentence. The best Scott could do was try to get on experimental drug trials till someone found a cure, which most experts put at years, even decades, away. The prospects were bleak, but Scott was hopeful. He didn't want to give up, he wanted to fight. At the time he told me, not a lot of people knew Scott was ill, but he wanted to go public with his condition in hopes of drawing awareness. He also didn't have health insurance, making his situation that much more dire. So we called Harriet Spizziri, who lived in Skokie, just north of Chicago, who, when she wasn't running a renegade theatre, was a suburban mom. She was also the first call many 20-something theatre artists made if they had an adult question like, say, how do I file my taxes, or, in Scott's case, how do I get health insurance so I can avoid a hasty death at the hands of a mysterious disease. Harriet's help was invaluable— she was able to finagle insurance for Scott (still not quite sure how she did that). She also offered help in the form of advice from her dad, who, weirdly, was involved in top secret medical trials to find a cure for AIDS. I was struck dumb—how lucky, that we might stumble across the first ever cure for AIDS at the time we need it most. Scott was less convinced and called Harriet's claim "news of the weird." Turns out he was right. Harriet never mentioned her dad, or his miracle cure, again.

Despite Scott's existential fight for survival, or perhaps because of it, our efforts to find a home for *Marvin's Room* doubled. The play was Scott's baby, literally, his raison d'être. He wanted to see it produced. It became a kind of mission and, frankly, a race against the clock. The next most notable theatre in Chicago was The Goodman. I knew the artistic director there, Bob Falls, but only in passing. My more direct contact was with David Petrarca, who had been hired as Associate Artistic Director a year or so before. David was about my age. He had been a Theatre Communications Group Directing Fellow—chosen from a slew of candidates who applied every year and were appointed to different posts at regional theatres across the country. When that tenure ended, Falls kept him on and gave him a promotion.

I reasoned that Petrarca might be a foot in the door. David and I had mingled recently at a bar or party sometime after a show, where he told me I should give him a call, we should get together. Now was my chance to take him up on that. So I phoned David, told him I had a project that might interest The Goodman, and we set a meeting. David asked me to get him a script in the meantime, which I did. I printed a copy, hustled down to the Goodman and hand delivered it. And a few days later we met. Unfortunately, David had not yet read the play, but he promised he would. He asked if I was attached as director and I told him yes, I was. We chatted about this and that and parted ways. And then I waited. I can't remember the exact order of the next events, but about a week later, Scott phoned to say he'd received a call from David, who told him he—David—was looking for a play to direct in his new role at the Goodman, and he wanted that play to be *Marvin's Room*.

I was speechless for a moment, and then my head went dizzy. Once I recovered, I asked Scott his thoughts and he told me, understandably, that it would be a really pretty hard gig to turn down. And not just because it was the Goodman, but because there was a very real possibility he might not be around much longer.

I asked Scott if he would let me try to see if Victory Gardens Theatre was interested. He agreed, albeit half-heartedly. The drop-off from Steppenwolf or the Goodman to Victory Gardens—a respectable but less attractive and mid-sized theatre—was pretty steep. It was a choice between national attention versus regional. Regardless, I went to Sandy Shinner, then associate artistic director of Victory Gardens. Sandy, who was also Scott's friend, had been at our little reading at Steppenwolf and was a huge fan of the play. If fact, while Scott and I were shopping it around to the Goodman and Steppenwolf, she had been lobbying to let Victory Gardens have the premiere production. And I would be guaranteed the director's seat. But Dennis Zaceck, Victory Garden's artistic director, was not ready to plan his season, and he wasn't going to make any exceptions with *Marvin's Room*.

So that was that. I was out of options. I had no other contacts with any other equity companies in the city. I met with Scott and told him to take Petrarca's offer. He had no choice. The play needed to get out into the world. Sad but relieved, Scott agreed.

I didn't speak to Scott for a while after that. Not because we weren't still friends, but because it was awkward. Scott would now be devoting most of his energies to the Goodman production. That and fighting to stay alive.

In and around this time, I had my experience with *The Grapes of Wrath*. Working with Scott on *Marvin's Room*—when he wrote his first draft—took place between the Chicago and London productions of *Grapes* in 1988-89, so I was kept busy. It was actually my experience getting burned on *Marvin's Room* that inspired me to write my first play, an adaptation of Mark Harris' baseball-centric novel *Bang the Drum Slowly*, which premiered at Next. Up until that point, playwriting was a mystery, something meant for a rarified breed of exceptional artists who knew how to make a story and entertain people by magically putting words, sentences, scenes and whole acts together into a cohesive whole. It was never something I thought I could do. Until I watched Scott. Day after day, coming to my apartment with fresh scenes he had written the night before was a revelation. Of course, the craft of writing is not easy, and I would find that out soon enough. But *Marvin's Room* was the experience that got me off my butt and thinking that maybe the average Joe, schlepping around in his t-shirt and jeans, might stand a chance of creating something wonderful out of thin air.

Another impetus to start writing was the realization that,

as a director, I had so little control over the projects I wanted to pursue. However many hours I put into *Marvin's Room*, or whatever influence I had on that play, it was never my play to begin with. Getting that project ripped away inspired me to never let that happen again. I needed to find a better, safer and more practical way to do the business of art. In this manner, writing *Bang the Drum Slowly* was an act of rebellion and defiance. I needed control over the things I created.

And yet another benefit of watching Scott write was the understanding that he was using his skills as an actor to make his stories come to life. I touched on this earlier, but *Marvin's Room* is where I first understood that the best writers were at one time actors. Creating dialogue is difficult coming at it from the outside, as a director. But if you put yourself in the shoes of the characters and get them to talk to one another—if you act out the story while writing—well, it's not easy, but it certainly helps. This takes the skill of an actor, or improvisor. Or both.

Marvin's Room opened at The Goodman Theatre in 1990 to rave reviews—as I thought it would. It was immediately picked up by Hartford Stage, and then Playwrights Horizons in New York, after which it moved to the Minetta Lane Theater, where it ran for seven months. Later, it was optioned by Producer Scott Rudin and became an Oscar nominated major motion picture starring Meryl Streep, Diane Keaton and Leonardo DiCaprio.

After the dust settled, Scott and I went back to being friends. This was around 1992, and his disease had progressed. The last time I saw Scott, he was at his apartment on Lakeview Avenue, just north of Belmont. He preferred home to the hospital, even though that put him far from the immediate care he might require at any moment. Ironically, *Marvin's Room* had finally given Scott the financial security he looked for all his life, but he didn't have much of an appetite for spending money. Though he did show off a new cabinet he had just purchased, which was meant to look old, in the fashion of the day. He joked that his sister was perplexed anyone would pay good money for something that looked so crappy. He lie there on his brand new leather couch, under a blanket, his cheeks hollowed out. He apologized for not being able to see *The Song of Jacob Zulu*, which had just opened at Steppenwolf, and we talked about maybe working on our next project. But we both kind of knew that was not going to happen anytime soon. He was so exhausted he could barely put pen to paper. He complained that the Hollywood folks who had bought the rights to *Marvin's Room* were taking such a damn long time getting the film off the ground. He didn't have much hope he would see the finished product.

He was right on that count. Scott passed away on November 7th, 1992, a full four years before the movie would be released. And by the way, Larry Sloan, who had introduced us, died from AIDS complications two and a half years later. The whole AIDS epidemic did quite a number on our little corner of the theatre world. It's hard to look back on that time without remembering the loss.

I often think about Scott and what he would have created had he survived. He was so incredibly gifted, and also fast, able to churn out one scene after another effortlessly. He never took playwriting or theatre too seriously, and that kept him from treating anything as precious. He had so many ideas it was hard to keep up with him. When Scott first pitched me *Marvin's Room*, he had three or four other stories waiting in the wings, ready to go in rapid succession. I remember that *Marvin's Room* was the best of them, but the others were pretty damn good too. I imagine that if Scott had lived he would have moved to L.A. and probably become a successful screenwriter or television show-runner and creator. That's what we had dreamt about way back when. I think he probably would have been one of the best, maybe as good as David E. Kelley or the great Norman Lear. He was that good. And that prolific.

And I miss him terribly.

6

There Will be Obstacles

"Always do what you are afraid to do."
— Ralph Waldo Emerson

"Every artist was first an amateur."
— also Ralph Waldo Emerson

THE FIRST FOUR DAYS of rehearsal we stayed around the table, reading the script. Stopping, starting. Asking questions and talking about the play, characters, the meaning of lines as translated from the original Russian. Yasen was well versed in *Seagull*, and all things Chekhov, and he was never without an answer. I mentioned the biography I had read, telling the room I was amazed there were so many incidents from Chekhov's real life that made it into the script. And I felt the director in me creeping out. I must have sounded like a braggart, the good student, but honestly, I love doing the damn research. I always have, and I do as much as I can no matter the project or what role I have in it. As a writer, it's a given I need to know the period, background, environment, socio-economic situations of the characters and story, or I stand the risk of hitting false notes, or worse, getting lost in the story. If I ever get writer's block, the first thing I do is go back to research and that usually pulls me out of it. As a director, it's imperative I know more than anybody in the room about the world of the play (or film as the case may be). More often than not, in fact, I over-research. And I did this with *Seagull* as well. In these table read discussions, I couldn't stop myself talking and having opinions that sometimes ran contrary to Yasen's. Before long I felt I had to tamp that down a bit. Putting myself in the director's shoes, again, I appreciate the actor who will sublimate their will to the greater good of the production, and the production can only be clearly communicated when all artistic choices are funneled through the director. So I reigned in, and told myself I needed to stay true to Yasen's vision—whatever that may be—of what we were doing. And actually? That felt pretty damn good. I had my little part I needed to worry about and nothing more.

When we moved away from the table and got up on our feet, things felt natural, even seamless. No one was looking at me like I didn't belong there. So far, so good. My game plan for staging, putting the character on his feet, was to lose the script as soon as possible so I could play out scenes unencumbered. But I was too nervous to commit to that right off the bat, so I kept hold of my pages just in case. And it looked like most everyone else had the same idea. The entire cast except, I think, for Namir and Lusia held their scripts but never looked at them (Namir and Luisa held the scripts *and* looked at them). Here's where I hoped muscle memory might kick in, moving and talking at the same time to help me remember lines. But that turned out not to be the case. The minute I put my script down my brain fell out of my skull. I felt a little panic and no matter how many times we ran a scene, I'd be searching for my lines, for a single word that would trigger all else—character, intention, motivation. And even if I knew the correct intention, I wouldn't allow myself to paraphrase for fear of cementing the wrong words. I needed to be exact, precise, especially now, early on. Otherwise, I felt, I was dissing Chekhov, the playwright, and Yasen, who adapted his words. And of course my fellow actors, who needed to hear the correct cue. But this desire for precision, for perfection, turned into a seemingly out of reach challenge that I had not anticipated.

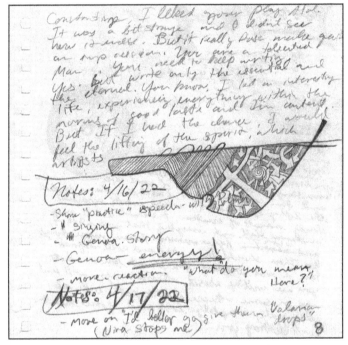

One tactic I used to memorize lines was writing them down. Over and over again.

As a director, I'm used to a rehearsal process which looks something like this: Week One is table work and discussions about character, intentions, themes, research, etc. Week Two and the first part of Week Three are devoted to staging and review of staging. There's a free flow and exchange of thoughts as director and ensemble find their characters and build on the director's vision. Once the entire play is staged, there's a period of time when the actors sort of know their lines but struggle and call out for help from stage management. This is Week Three and a half to Week Four and a half. It's primarily devoted to running, getting notes and working out the knots of problem moments. Weeks One, Two and the last part of Four I'm generally fine with as a director, in that these are necessary rehearsals packed with inspiration and creativity. These are the days of collaboration and exploration, when things are discovered and the secrets inherent in the play are revealed. It's that wonky section that starts the end of Week Three that sends me round the bend and gets me wondering why directors just don't skip town and take a week off. Because this period is almost entirely devoted to actors getting their fucking lines down. It's boring and tedious, sort the equivalent of a computer processing all the data it's been asked to remember—while a programmer waits, twiddling thumbs. It's the equivalent of staring at the spinning beachball of death while your laptop uploads a large file.

For actors, usually, this period is unavoidable and necessary. Ironically, happily, in our production we did not have this problem. Perhaps it was time off from the pandemic, or the extreme professionalism of the *Seagull* ensemble, or maybe it was in anticipation of the challenge ahead. But our cast was hyper-prepared. And I, too, proudly held my own. In fact, by the end of Week Two, I was rock solid, still seeing the lines before me at the front of my brain, but getting them out in a halfway believable fashion. That didn't mean the obsession with remembering lines evaporated. I still had Bob on the brain. It wasn't enough for me to just know the lines. To avoid Bob's fate, I needed to be able to say my lines doing cartwheels. I needed to make this part of my process bulletproof. Meanwhile I was missing home, missing my other projects. And I was reminded that actors actually have a lot of down time to... I don't know, to...what? Do what exactly? In my case, way back when, it was my day job that filled the hours not on stage. Then when I was making enough as an actor (essentially my stint doing *Grapes*) I was, well, farting around. Now, with years of pretty much continuous work in my rear view mirror, I had gotten out of the habit of just farting around. I tried to work on writing projects I had in development—things I would return to once I was back home—but that's not an easy thing to do with a pending opening fright-night looming. I had a laser beam focus on this challenge. Everything else felt like a distraction. Any spare time I had, I devoted to thinking and breathing Yevgeny Sergeyevich Dorn.

And, as rehearsal proceeded—getting into the second and third weeks of rehearsal—the good doctor was shaping up nicely, I thought. Later, long after we had opened the play, I talked to Yasen about his memory of the rehearsal process, and he told me it looked to him like I was coming at the part with a great deal of confidence—a lot more than he expected. And, he said, that as opening night approached, he thought I had turned into myself and lost some of that confidence. I think this is an accurate assessment of what actually happened. Early on in the rehearsal process, I felt pretty good about what I was doing, despite the fact that, after Yasen's initial thumbs up (after that first read-through), he gave me little to no encouragement.

Now, I don't think Yasen was unhappy with my work at any time during the process. In fact, I know from conversations I had with him later, he wasn't. I think his silence was more a matter of his hands-off directing style. I didn't get a lot of praise, and occasionally I would get a gentle suggestion to take my character in this direction or that. And this was okay. It felt very collaborative. I had a say in the shaping of this man called Dorn, and Yasen was excited to meet me half way.

During one of our first rehearsals I was strumming a prop guitar, one that Eli Newman, the actor playing the serf, Yakov, would use throughout the show for incidental music. I had long ago taught myself guitar and played it infrequently over the years. I did what we in the non-business world call a little "noodling" from time to time. I could pick up a guitar and pluck out a song from, oh, perhaps a canon of a dozen standards I'd learned, and sound halfway decent. Apparently Yasen heard me "noodle" that one day and after rehearsal he phoned me and asked if I wouldn't mind making it part of Dorn's character. Dorn has these moments in the play when he just randomly sings, or mumbles, a little tune here and there. I liked these moments. They seemed like a natural thing that occurs in real life—someone subconsciously breaks into song, then stops. Very spontaneous, very Chekhovian. And an interesting challenge. This was Yasen's solution. Rather than have Dorn stumble-mumble into a short musical phrase, I would simply pick up a guitar and break into a full blown song.

Happy to do it. Anything to distract from actual acting.

Yasen was also keen on developing the relationship between Dorn and Polina, the woman with whom my character was secretly having an affair. Sandra Marquez, playing Polina, was eager to grow this relationship too, and it was from this that I started thinking about my relationships with all the characters on stage, and I noticed this: I had at least a little bit of a scene, or exchange, with every single one of the other ten characters in the play. I thought this was amazing, and it couldn't have been an accident. Chekhov must have done this consciously because I noticed as I tracked all the roles that they, too, had at least one interaction with all the other characters on stage. That's got to add up to scores of individual relationships.

Jeff Perry and Yasen often compared what we were doing to jazz, as opposed to classical music, I guess, or popular music. We were an ensemble of actors in a play, just like musicians in a group or a combo. In jazz, musicians learn a skill—their instrument—and when they play a song, they agree on a key. They learn a standard, or whatever, and play it together, but then they stray from the rigid notes on a staff to groove and bop as needed, until it's time to meet up at a certain measure or verse. In this way, we as actors agree on a script, then the tone and attack of that script. We play the notes—or the words—but internally we give ourselves the freedom to explore, to jam, to free up what we are doing. And we're allowed to do this as long as we all meet up at the same place and check in with each other from time to time.

Jazz—or blues music—is how Steppenwolf has always described its style. Terry Kinney likes to say it's more rock and roll. And he may be right. It might come closest to defining what some refer to as the "Chicago" style of acting. I cut my teeth in Chicago, and whatever Steppenwolf was doing, the rest of the theatre crowd in Chicago tried to do, so this way of approaching a play wasn't unfamiliar to me. It was what I did at all those non-equity theatres when I was acting way back when. When Yasen saw confidence in me in the first couple weeks, this was why: it was all coming back. It was like finding my sea legs through blocking and using that—my movement, the posture, etc.—to inform who I was and how I related to the other characters. Pretty much the first day we were on our feet, I found Dorn's walk, his physical nature. He was a peacock, I decided, and he led with his chest. He didn't just walk, he preened, he strutted, with long strides that said "Look at me look at me look at me." Everything about him started with his libido. The guitar helped. As staged, playing the instrument was practically the first thing I did when I ran—not walked—on stage for my first entrance. The arresting strum of a C major chord, directed right at Polina, announced who I was. After a brief scene in which we flirted secretly, we were joined by the rest of the ensemble. By then, I was able to relax into the role. The next ten minutes I had a few lines here and there, but mostly all I needed to do was listen. These were moments, I decided, Dorn was taking in information about the world around him and the friends and strangers who populated it. Was he, like Chekhov, getting ready to write a play influenced by all he experienced? Yes, I thought. And this gave me a bedrock of motivation I exploited from day one.

It was about this time I realized something else. What I knew about acting, and how I went about crafting my performance, had much less to do with the brief time, many years before, when I was an actor. Because in between my last performance ever and now, I had been directing and writing scores of plays. And while I was doing that, I was constantly putting myself in the shoes of my characters. Many times, in the privacy of my own home and away from the rehearsal room, as a writer. I would act out every role so I could better understand my characters. As a director, this empathetic approach helped me communicate my notes to actors. And I found myself giving the same notes time and again, across many productions, over three decades. These include:

- Punch the ends of your lines. Bring them up in pitch and volume, otherwise you will not be heard and energy will be lost.

- Make sure you have an intention or action behind every line, no matter how small or insignificant that line may seem.

- Don't be afraid to take the stage when it's your turn. And be generous when it's time to give it up.

- Come on stage with energy. In other words, when you enter, *take stage*.

- Always listen actively.

- If any moment feels false, find out why and fix it.

- Know the character's subtext and play it.

- Wear your character as lightly as you wear a hat.

This last bit was advice given by the late, great Byrne Piven, a Chicago actor and fixture in the '80s and '90s. Byrne was a barrel chested, bearded, self-important man with a fog-horn voice who, aptly, wore a Greek fisherman's cap forever cocked oh-so-dramatically to one side. Everyone in Chicago knew Byrne, who, with his lovely wife Joyce, started the Piven Theatre Workshop in Evanston and trained the likes of John and Joan Cusack, Lily Taylor, and Aidan Quinn. When I first came to Chicago and was looking for actual theatre work, Byrne and Joyce gave me my first job as an instructor, and I'll always be grateful for that. They did not have to employ me, they could have found a more qualified teacher, but they knew I needed work. And I guess they saw something in me and they gave me a leg up.

"Wear the character as lightly as you wear your hat." was one of Byrne principal instructions, and had to do with not letting one's character work overpower a performance and obscure the honesty mined by the actor. If the audience is watching the technique rather listening to the story, then you are failing. You are drawing unneeded attention to the artifice.

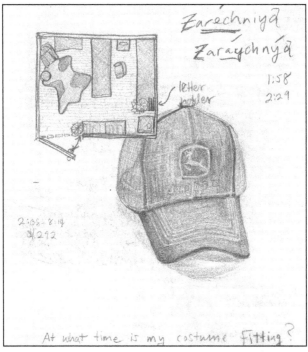

I was overcome with homesickness every once in a while. This page shows a ground plan of my home office in L.A., which I drew from memory.

These "rules" are things I collected—subconsciously or otherwise—over the years (I guess), first as an actor, and then as a director and a writer. And not one is particularly more important than another. And they are all pretty much at the core of every modern day philosophy or approach to good, solid technique.

So I was feeling pretty good about the way things were progressing in rehearsal. But also dreading the passage of time because that meant getting closer to performing before an audience. Despite my ease in getting back on the horse (horse, bike, whatever), and feeling safe and comfortable around my fellow actors, I was still unsure about how I would perform in front of a crowd.

And maybe that's about the time when, during the fourth week, Yasen says he noticed my confidence slipping.

7

How Soon is Now?

"Ever tried. Ever failed. No matter. Try again. Fail again. Fail better."

— Samuel Beckett, *Wrostward Ho*

IT HIT ME around the first or second week of rehearsal that there was another reason my acting chops might be coming back so quickly, and that was the brief time I spent doing improv comedy. I realize improv is a natural part of any professional actor's eduction, and also many amateur performer's education. It's a tool that is used in company workshops and self-help seminars to the point of cliché. Improv is ubiquitous and annoying, especially when done badly.

But long ago, back in the Stone Age, when I graduated from college, improv was king. It meant Saturday Night Live, the Second City Revue in Chicago and Second City TV. Improv, especially by way of Chicago's Second City, seemed the quickest way to fame and fortune. For us serious artists interested in theatre only, we still found our way to Viola Spolin, whose son Paul Sills was one of the founders of the Compass Players, which became Second City.

Producer Bernie Sahlins and Chicago Theatre mentor Sheldon Patinkin were also instrumental in the start of Second City. These two rock solid Chicago theatre titans would eventually become my good friends.

My pal, Gregg Mierow, and me performing a Spolin exercise at Lawrence. He and I would travel to in Madison right after graduation, where we joined the Ark Repertory Theatre.

Back when I was in college, I only cared about Viola Spolin and her instructional book *Improvisation for the Theatre.* My college mates and I studied that book, did games from it and formed an improv group that took the practice of improv very seriously. We weren't in it for the laughs, we were interested in the thought behind the practice and what it revealed about the nature of acting. How do you make good theatre without a script? How does improvisation help an actor carve out an actual performance?

When I graduated from Lawrence and decided I wasn't going to decide what I was going to do for a while, I moved to Madison with a couple pals, Gregg Mierow and Karl Kramer, to hang out for a while. We sort of bummed around and deliberately avoided making life decisions. We certainly worried about money. It was the middle of a national recession, and work of any kind was hard to find. Eventually I got a job at a Walgreens stocking shelves for something like four dollars an hour, and I also sold plasma at the local blood letting clinics. Pretty pathetic stuff. In my spare time (of which I had a lot) I vegged out at the University of Wisconsin student union on Lake Mendota. One day, I spotted an ad in the Isthmus, the Madison free weekly calling for people to audition for a new improv company called The Ark Repertory Theatre.

I showed the ad to my friend Gregg, also interested in theatre, and the two of us said "What the hell, let's go for it." And we were cast! Not a mean feat, actually, since, as far as I could tell, everyone who showed up for the audition (about six of us) was cast.

And we were unspeakably bad. Gregg and I actually held our own, as did another cast member, Lynn Baker, who was talented, tall, dark, and statuesque, with a shock of 1980s Joan Jett black, curly hair. But the others in the group struggled. Most had never set foot on stage, let alone acted in an improv group. Our fearless leader and founder, Elaine Eldridge Kern, was a recent Madison transplant and a waifish, throw-back hippie with no money, just a dream and a bunch of free labor from a motley crew of fresh co-eds and recent grads. Elaine was pretty much learning improv as she went along, and though Gregg and I knew only the basics, we certainly knew a lot more than she.

As our opening night approached—a free gig playing the rowdy Madison Rathskeller—Lynn pulled Gregg and me aside in a panic and voiced what we already knew: the show was going to be a disaster unless we did something. She knew a couple pretty good actors. It was late in the game, but maybe they could join the group.

It took some doing, but Elaine, who was a bit territorial and self-destructive (deadly combination), finally agreed to see Lynn's friends, Evan Gore and Joan Cusack. We invited them to one of our rehearsals and the cast performed a few improv games. I thought we did terribly, but I remember Evan, dressed in the fashion of early Elvis Costello, and Joan, who could've easily passed for Boy George, were pretty entertained. Beforehand, Lynn had told us that Joan had a couple movie credits under her belt, and I was pretty impressed. I didn't know anybody who had been in a major motion picture. One of Joan's films, *My Bodyguard*, had just come out. The other, *Sixteen Candles*, was about to be released.

After our little group had embarrassed ourselves failing at Spolin games, Elaine invited Joan and Evan to come up and take part, and they dove right in. And they were sharp, and witty and downright brilliant. It was instantly clear these two were by far superior, more evolved and talented than anyone in the group. After we finished, and we were all floating on that improv high one only gets from nailing a series of bonafide laughs, we all looked to Elaine and waited for a reaction. Surely she would not waste any time inviting these two geniuses into the group.

But of course that wasn't in the cards. Elaine hemmed and hawed, and said something like "I think I'm gonna—I think I need to—I think I—let me think it over," and then, "Thank you for playing in our little sandbox," or some bullshit. But after a some cajoling and veiled threats from Lynn, Gregg and myself that we would walk, Elaine agreed to cast Evan and Joan… on a trial basis. Which didn't last long. Joan and Evan brought their own friends into the fold: Jeff Kahn, Mark Herzog, Doug Rand, and Holly Wortell. The few bad apples in the group left, and not long after, we had a pretty kick-ass company. We performed at local bars for tips. We all set up the stage and the lights every week. We started out playing to a handful of friends. Word got out eventually, and before long we were playing to sold-out houses.

I mentioned briefly the high that one experiences at the end of a set or a show. I need to elaborate on that because it's a performance high like no other. The immediate gratification that comes from making something up in the moment that's perfect and spot on while on the tight rope, working without a net, is like hitting a bullseye on a faraway dart board. It's like cracking a whip and killing a fly midair. Everyone's waiting for it, and the laughter confirms your moment of honesty, it hits you like a load of endorphins released from the brain. In fact, that is exactly what's going on, scientifically speaking, and though you're on stage and need to stay in character (i.e. not laugh), the joy is still there, as are the constant laughs that come while offstage watching your fellow improv partners go to town.

Looking back on it now, I think that time in Madison was one of the reasons I felt so free and without fear in those first rehearsals of *Seagull*. Perhaps that kind of fearlessness has always been a part my process, whether I was aware of it or not. I've always been of the mind that, for better or worse, you have to put yourself out there if you're going after something everyone else wants. That was true then, it's true today. But I also think, dialing up the proverbial bicycle again, getting on the stage is really something you never forget. The tools one uses to connect with another, to connect with the audience, to take stage, make an entrance, know when to get off, the skills that call on the spontaneous self to try this or that and see if it works, or not—all these things I learned in those few months, early on, doing improv in bars when I was 21 and living in Madison...

The original Ark members regrouped in Chicago to form An Impulsive Thing. We performed to crowds in bars for about a year before, one by one, we split off to pursue other dreams. Left to right: Mark Herzog, Holly Wortell, Bonnie Hunt, Andy Miller, Jeff Kahn, Evan Gore, John Grippentrog, Gregg Mierow, me (bearded). Photo: Suzanne Plunkett.

... And later in Chicago. I was the first to disembark The Ark and try my luck in the City of the Big Shoulders. The others in the group stayed behind, mostly to finish school at UW Madison.[8] But eventually we all ended up in Chicago, or rather, The Land of a Thousand Improv Groups. We called our own new group An Impulsive Thing, and added a couple new members, including

---

8. Students of the improv history will know The Ark was also where Chris Farley got his start.

John Grippentrog and Bonnie Hunt, and we were on our way. We played in bars on the north side of the city and, just like in Madison, started out playing to a smattering of friends, and gradually gained a following. It didn't take long, though, for the group to splinter. At the time, I was more interested in traditional theatre. Evan Gore, Holly Wantuch and Bonnie Hunt were eventually recruited by Second City. Joan, the superstar of the group, was picked up by SNL. Jeff Kahn partnered with Ben Stiller and went off to New York to create *The Ben Stiller Show*. And Mark Herzog moved to L.A. to start a production company, which he runs to this day.[9]

It strikes me as funny, though, that the Chicago performing community has always been this unique place that is equal parts improv and scripted theatre. Second City and the Improv Olympics came up right along side The Goodman and Steppenwolf, and they fed off one another. There aren't many examples of performers moving easily between one medium and the other—in fact, they co-existed like two planets in the same solar system, a part from one another but dependent on and influenced by one another's movements. If a performer did one discipline, it was nearly impossible for them to do both. Just one took up too much time and focus. But still, they co-existed and could not ignore one another. There is always a bit of improv—or rock and roll if you will—in Steppenwolf's work. And Second City, and their competitors—places like Friends of the Zoo and The Practical Theatre (Julia Louis-Dreyfus' first artistic home) became more structured as time went on, more like genuine theatre companies. It's quite

---

9. Herzog and Company produced many of the CNN documentaries seen today: The '60s, '70s etc. series. Mark was instrumental in giving me support on my first documentaries, *On Tiptoe* and *On a Note of Triumph*. It's safe to say that without Mark's help I would have never had a career in TV and film.

possible that Chicago acting has something to do with the longstanding, subconscious, symbiotic relationship between these two styles of performing.

* * *

The last week in the rehearsal room, every day we ran the play from beginning to end and then sat for notes. Yasen kept true to his process and remained pretty much hands off. I listened to what he told other actors and decided he knew what he was doing. I could only assume his advice to me was as solid. Still, he was short on compliments. But I know from decades in theatre that this has more to do with directors having lots on their minds. Yasen was not only in charge of turning out good performances, he was opening a brand new performance space with his play and responsible for delivering a spectacular production. Based on feedback from actors I've directed in the past, I know I myself can be pretty short on compliments without realizing it. For some actors, this is unnerving. Others have thick skins. They have the confidence to stick to the path they're on till otherwise directed. I've worked with both kinds of actors and have to say I appreciate the self sufficient ones more. Less hand-holding means more time for the big picture.

The end of the last week culminated with what's known as the "designer run." This is when the design staff are invited to take a look at the work so far. "Designer run," though, is a misnomer, because pretty much the entire backstage crew and most of the theatre staff are invited as well. This would essentially be our first audience.

And I was scared shitless. Yes, by this time I knew what I was doing, theoretically. But the lines were still. Not. Sticking! And that pissed me off, majorly. Goddammit, I'd started memorizing a month and a half before rehearsal began. And my part, honestly, compared to other roles in the play? Not that big. That last week, when we were running the show over and over, I got through only one out of five runs without calling for a line. Sure, other actors were calling for lines too, but did they have a history of stage fright? The rest of the cast were stage veterans and knew their own strengths and limitations. They were pros; I was not.

I really needed to believe I could do this. I needed this designer run to go well for me.

When it was time to start, Yasen said a few words to the group, made a couple jokes—I laughed with all the others, but I had no idea what he said.

And then we started… And honestly? I don't remember a thing about it. I focused on my lines and leaned into muscle memory. And that was about it. I remember Marcus Doshi, the lighting designer (whom I'd worked with as a director, on *Lindiwe* at S.T.C. a couple years before), laughed giddily during my first scene with Polina. Why? The scene wasn't that funny. Or was it? Or was he laughing at the sight of his former boss making a fool out of himself on stage? Never mind, I couldn't let it affect my performance. The rest of the run I was more or less on automatic pilot, tense with the fear that I was going to slip up. If I managed to pass myself off as a reasonably believable human being, I was fine with that. I did finish without calling for a line, and that, in and of itself, was a win as far as I was concerned.

In the short note session to the cast that followed, Yasen commended us all on a first run and someone—I can't remember who — joked that Chekhov was a bitch to act. Everyone laughed. Yeah, I guess so. My entire performance felt only halfway there and so far from finished. And yes, Chekhov, it turns out, is indeed a bitch to act.

Why?

Many reasons. But most likely his understanding of the complexity of the human condition, which is also the reason why his plays have survived. Chekhov characters behave like real people. And yet, in another respect, they are unlike anyone anybody has ever met, or even seen on stage in plays by other playwrights. Chekhov's plays have characters who behave the way real people do, including all the parts that are inexplicable and puzzling. Intentions and beat changes happen randomly and without reason. Just like real life. Mostly, the characters in Chekhov's plays never get what they want, no matter how hard they try. Just like real life.

Every other playwright in the world, it seems, famous or otherwise (and especially those writing today) try hard to make sense out of the chaos that is real life. Characters are drawn from people with clear, unwavering ambitions and desires. Their paths are linear for the most part, their goals, subtextual and otherwise, are clear. The clashes they render are warranted, relatable and understandable. And every character whim and choice is manipulated by the playwright to express a particular theme and emotion that has an intellectual payoff.

Chekhov is the opposite of that. Goals are left unattained, people capriciously contradict themselves and no one is ever satisfied. Politics are non-existent, and when they do appear, they quickly evaporate like an illusion and remain frustratingly unresolved.[10] No one is right and no one is wrong; everyone is right and

---

10. This may have been a result of the political environment in which Chekhov was writing. Plays were heavily censored and bucking up against the Tsar's

everyone is wrong. Dialogue is alternatingly naturalistic and then all at once self-conscious. Non-sequiturs abound.

And yet, this uneven and elusive style of writing is endlessly interesting. Particularly for an actor. Simple characters in transparent plays are probably easier to master, but equally problematic in bringing to life night after night. With Chekhov, there are seemingly endless possibilities to go about playing every single line. This is what I discovered in rehearsal. And because Chekhov employs so many group scenes, this gives every actor permission to fill in the blanks of what is going on with their character whether he or she is speaking or silent. And this is wonderful because it throws every actor in the role of a collaborator. The actor is forced to invent action from whole cloth, flesh out character, and in essence become a co-writer with Chekhov, with the given director, with the other actors on stage. In any Chekhov play—well produced— the actor has agency and creative license. The actor is singular and distinct, an essential part of the finished product.

---

political dogma was strictly forbidden

8

——— ⋅৩৶৹⋅ ———

The Empty Space

"We create our buildings and then they create us.
Likewise, we construct our circle of friends and our com-
munities and then they construct us."

— Frank Lloyd Wright

FOR OVER TEN YEARS, Steppenwolf had been planning to build a new theatre space to live right alongside its existing 500 seat proscenium. It all started with Martha Lavey, artistic director from 1997 to 2017, who proposed a new space that was meant to be a virtual duplicate of the already existing theatre. The idea was that if Steppenwolf had a hit play—which was often in the early 2000s— the company could keep it running concurrently with whatever was scheduled for the regular season. This scheme, however, had its drawbacks. What happened, for instance, if the theatre stopped producing hit shows? Also, many in the ensemble scratched their head at spending millions of dollars on a theatre that was essentially a carbon copy of what we already had.

Among these doubters was director and ensemble member Anna Shapiro, who took over for Martha Lavey in 2017. One of her first actions as A.D. was to tear up the plans for the proscenium theatre and reimagine a completely different space, something that would give the ensemble a distinct theatrical alternative. What she proposed was a 400 seat in-the-round theatre. This became instantly controversial with the ensemble, made up primarily of actors, most of whom had never acted in the round. To be fair, the in-the-round theatre has many critics, not just actors, but directors and designers, and audiences too. There are, in fact, only a few dozen (out of hundreds) professional "island" stages in the entire country, the most prominent being Arena Stage in Washington, D.C., Marriott Lincolnshire in Rosewood, Illinois, and Circle in Square on Broadway. After a brief popularity in the 60s and 70s, in-the-round mostly fell out of favor, and for all the obvious reasons: audience members staring at one another from across the way, less opportunities for spectacular production designs, acoustics challenges. Steppenwolf actors were primarily concerned about being heard and having their backs to half the audience. But there were advantages to the arena configuration, specifically for a theatre like Steppenwolf. At 400 seats spread out over four sides, every audience member would be very close to the stage, which meant an extraordinarily intimate relationship with the players.

Steppenwolf gained its reputation by way of a sweaty, visceral, in-your-face, close-up acting style. Ensemble member playwright/actor Tracy Letts (and author of *August: Osage County*), who had been a part of the team researching the new design, was a strong advocate for in-the-round. According to Yasen, who was also part of that team, Tracy said he wanted the audience to "feel the spit coming from the actors mouths."

I have had two plays produced in-the-round—both of which

I'd written and one I directed—at Circle in the Square on Broadway. And I'm a big fan. I love the proximity of the audience to the actors. I actually love that people were looking right across at the other half of the audience throughout the production. It reminds them they are not alone, that they are, in fact, in a church-like setting amongst others in their community, listening to and experiencing the same story. I love always being reminded I am watching a play. I love that you can come back and see a show two, three, four times and, depending on where you sit, experience a slightly different version of the same production. For me, it makes theatre more alive and special, something happening now and in this moment, at this time.

What's more, technology has advanced and solved some of the sonic and scenic issues long associated with in-the-round. At Circle, we had scenery coming up, using hydraulics, from a trap room that was the size of the stage itself. We also lowered set pieces down from the light grid. Sound issues were managed by super flexible, high-tech floor mics that picked up dialogue and boosted them naturalistically to parts of the house that were temporarily disadvantaged by an actor whose back was turned.[11]

The construction of the Ensemble Theatre began in 2019, and was stopped temporarily by the pandemic. Then it was bravely restarted a couple months after most pandemic shut-downs, in defiance of that crisis. Construction workers forged ahead, adhering to strict Covid protocol, and they didn't miss a beat over the next two years. The target date for completion was spring of 2022, with the opening of *Seagull*.

---

11. Steppenwolf's *Seagull* did not employ this technique as the production staff felt the acoustics was so good we wouldn't need tech support. It wasn't.

* * *

The last day in the rehearsal room, the cast was together, gelling as an ensemble with no bad apples in sight. It's not easy to get an entire group together, moving in the same direction, and not have one asshole in the ranks. I told Yasen as much around this time. I credit it to him and his gentle, yet insistent, style of prodding actors towards their best performance. Though our production had a ways to go before it felt audience-ready.

On first glance, the finished theatre took your breath away. It was beautiful, a work of genius, really, and it had that "new home smell" to it, the scent of a place that was at the start of its journey in shelter management. It was visually stunning, inviting and warm. Sitting in the house felt equal parts comfortable and exciting—and more. The space was indeed, as we had hoped, very intimate. The back row was no more than 20 feet from the actors; the front row was right on top of them, at the lip of the stage, yet still separate, divided by a little moat, a line in the sand if you will, that kept audience from performer.

Aside from the circular paths that took the actors to four possible entrances, and the initial house-of-mirrors feeling it elicited, the backstage was, for all intents and purposes, friendly. On our first ever tour, the *Seagull* ensemble navigated offstage like we'd been there for years. The dressing rooms were voluminous, welcoming, though stark and minimalistic, offering no less, but no more then what was required. There was an ample kitchen with brand new appliances abutting an "open space" greenroom that felt ready for relaxing.

The whole tech theatre experience thing came rushing back to me. I staked out my place in the dressing room. Jeff Perry was my roommate.[12] The first thing I noticed when I walked into my dressing room was Dorn's costume. All that leather. First things first—I threw on my jacket. Nice. Then there was my hat, a fedora (remember, just like Indiana Jones). My rehearsal hat had been way-uncool: dopey and a little too big, which made me feel like an imposter. This one—the real one—felt pretty damn good. I turned, looked in the mirror. Oh, there's my guy. That's him: sexy doctor. Bit of a stretch, at least for me, but what a great disguise. The hat didn't just fit, it fit perfectly. It was exactly as I'd imagined.

Tech proceeded, as techs do: slowly. Though in this case, a lot less slowly than usual. At least the first part, Act I, had most of the difficult technical bits. Constantine's play within the play, as envisioned by Yasen and scenic designer Todd Rosenthal, was quite a production, with a circle disk that rose up a good five feet from stage level, carrying up with it Nina. Once at its height, it slowly turned while Nina recited Treplev's monologue. The creme de la creme, though, was an open flower petal fixed at the top of the grid, slowly coming down, wrapping itself around Nina and enclosing her in what looked like an enormous gilded cage (she's a seagull, get it?). It was a spectacular effect, and probably just what the production needed to show off the theatre's stagecraft potential.

Yasen and his crew amazingly whipped through this feat in the first four hours of rehearsal. After that, the tech doldrums set in and we spent the next three days slogging through the rest of

---

12. I had guessed correctly that he and I would be assigned to one another. Of course they're going to have the old guard—or rather the oldest guard—share a room. It's funny to me that when I first started working with Steppenwolf, ensemble members like Jeff Perry, Fran Guinan, and Rond Reed seemed so much older. I was the young upstart, they were the veterans. Now, at Steppenwolf events I'm always clumped in with the O.G.s.

the show. I have this theory that regardless of the days and hours allotted for tech rehearsals, any given production will use exactly the amount of time it's given. New theatre or no, the same rule applied here.

Caroline Neff performing Nina.

So, there was plenty of time to… run those fucking lines! And basically take a break from the rehearsal routine. Some actors hate techs, which are, after all, tedious and boring. As a director, I am hyper-aware about wasting actors' time while I finesse transitions and complicated tech sequences. My job in tech has everything to do with showing off my directing aplomb and little to do with advancing an actor's part in the collaboration. When I direct opera, we get what they call "light walkers" to stand in for performers during "dry techs" (techs without performers) when we set light cues. This gives singers much needed breaks to rest their voices and get ready for a rigorous run. I always thought this might be a good idea to try in the theatre world.

But here, doing *Seagull*, as an actor, I didn't mind the wait and downtime. I appreciated the break from the intense challenge of building a performance. I also loved hanging out and at least *pretending* to work. I was, after all, required to be there, getting paid, even though I was doing practically nothing. So I was feeling at least slightly useful, while getting to know the rest of the team, the backstage crew, the designers and their assistants, the running crew, the dressers, pretty much everyone. Jesus, it takes a lot of folks to make live theatre.

* * *

Chicago audiences are notoriously harsh critics. I'm not sure why. I've worked across the country in dozens of cities, including New York, and L.A., and I don't think there are any tougher customers. Part of the reason might be that Chicago audiences are used to excellence. It's been nearly 50 years since David Mamet, Steppenwolf, Remains and Wisdom Bridge jumped onto the scene. And before that, Chicago had the Goodman Theatre and Second City to crow about. Chicago audiences are spoiled and their standards are high. There have been many productions that started out in The Windy City and ended up on New York and London stages: *The Grapes of Wrath, August: Osage County, In the Belly of the Beast, Balm in Gilead, True West, Glengarry Glen Ross, Marvin's Room, Grease, Orphans,* Goodman's *The Iceman Cometh* and *Death of a Salesman. The Glass Menagerie* had its premiere at the Goodman in 1944! The bar is set high. And on any given night, there are many productions to choose from. Chicago has literally scores of theatres and shows running on any given night. Add to this the notion that most theatre people in New York still think of Chicago as the Second City, incapable of competing, a less-than platform for talent and creativity. Put all that together and you get an audience that is not only demanding of excellence, but harboring a little grudge. In Chicago, patrons seem to be saying, "If you can't give me better than New York, then get off the fucking stage."

Steppenwolf has a tradition of inviting Veterans of Foreign Wars to its first dress rehearsals. This was something started by Gary Sinise back in the early '80s, when he wanted to honor his brother-in-law, Mac, who fought in Vietnam. It's called simply, and aptly, Vet's Night. And it's a chance to run the show before a non-paying audience, and, of course, give back to the community. Vet's Night audiences are notoriously raucous, not your traditional playgoing crowd, given to huge, vocal responses. A simple kiss will elicit whoops and hollers. Any staged physical violence is met with an odd combination of cheers and outrage.

Vet's Night for *Seagull* was unfortunately pretty sparsely attended—something we would grow used to in subsequent performances. Covid-19 was still on the front of everyone's minds. Ticket sales throughout Chicago, at that time, for all live performances were anemic. And in a curious twist, many theater-goers would purchase tickets in advance and then not to show up. More on this later, but suffice it to say, this was definitely a downer for us actors—particularly in a circular space, where audience members are looking at the empty seats across the way and wondering if they bought tickets to a loser show. This was one thing we learned pretty quickly about our new space: it's a lot easier to hide a sparsely attended show in a proscenium theatre than in-the-round.

Vet's Night went... okay. It was similar to the designer run-through in that it felt like a white-knuckle event. At least for me. And probably for my fellow actors as well. I realized more than ever that the obsession with lines and memorization was not confined to me, and there were many in the cast who were struggling, particularly those with larger parts. So the performance on the whole was hit and miss. At one point, early in the third act, a cell phone went off. This is not an unusual event—it happens all the time in theatre, but audiences have gotten so used to it and the faux pas is usually detected by the offender and extinguished immediately. This cell phone, though, would not quit. It kept going until it felt like everyone in the theatre wanted to ring the neck of the son-of-a-bitch who wouldn't shut off their phone. Then it became clear the ringing was coming from on-stage. At long last, the culprit was revealed: An actor. On stage. Who had forgotten to leave their phone in the dressing room. ("The call is coming from inside the house!") Said actor let the phone ring in hopes (I guess) that no one would notice. The ringing eventually stopped. But then the caller redialed and it started all over again, at which point the actor, beyond irritation, took out the phone, slammed it against the floor and sent it flying off stage like a hockey puck.

Take that anecdotal incident away, however, the show still felt wobbly. Likewise, the audience reaction was in and out, here and there. I don't think they were overly-impressed, but their reactions helped in the way we had hoped, and guided us. They laughed in places we didn't expect, and didn't in places we thought they would. Not a lotta butts shifting in seats—good sign. Not much in the way of wandering attention. They were giving us invaluable information we would need to help us tell the story.

For my own part, despite the white-knuckling of it all, it was a personal triumph. I got through without fucking up. And I remembered all my lines. It was the minimum and the maximum of what I expected of myself.

The show the following night, though, was a whole other matter. I was terrified. Yes, another audience, but these folks paid to see the show. And, I guessed, they were probably more sophisticated. Would these people see through me to my inexperience, my rustiness? Would they be able to detect I wasn't really an actor, that I was, in fact, an imposter? But aren't all actors imposters? Really when you get down to it? They—we—are all pretending to be someone else.

Maybe there would be someone I knew in the audience. Despite all my efforts to keep my return to the stage a secret among my circle of friends and acquaintances, and despite having spent the past 25 years in L.A., I knew a lot of people in Chicago and suspected they would be attending this production at some time during the run.

Before the show, Jeff Perry asked me, "Are you the kind of person who wants to know someone is in the audience or does not want to know someone is in the audience?" And I thought, "Well, Jeff, I guess you just told me someone I know is going to be in the house watching the show tonight." I told Jeff, "No," and Jeff nodded affably and went about his business. I never, ever want to know there's someone I know in the audience. Even way back when in my early acting days this was the case. It makes me nervous beyond distraction. During the entire run of *Seagull*, I never encouraged friends to come and see me in the show.

So yes, I had to admit, despite promising myself I would kick the stage fright—and I was doing everything in my power to do that—I was still struggling. The thing I'd been fearing since the day I accepted this challenge had not disappeared. In fact, it may have gotten worse. I still had Bob in the back of my mind, of course—his knowing all his lines and then slowly forgetting until he was a puddle of fear on the stage floor, taking down his fellow actors with him, mumbling incoherently under the bright lights while everyone watched. And judged. That could be me. I could be him. That was a real possibility.

But I knew my lines, didn't I? I knew them backwards and forwards. I ran them a thousand times a day. But I didn't trust myself. There was still the ever present and real possibility I would let myself down. The theatre had entrusted me with this bit of stunt casting and I so wanted to prove to them I could pull it off and hold my own as a serious actor. Steppenwolf, above all else, was and is a home for great actors. It is an actor's theatre. I took that to heart, I wanted to honor it.

The second preview came and went. Again, I wasn't making any progress in fleshing out a performance. There was no art in what I was doing. I was treading water, merely getting through the show without disaster.

If this was a directing or writing issue, I would try to solve the problem in a practical manner. Writing, I concluded a long time ago, requires some talent, but mostly craft and discipline. Given the mechanics of story-telling, many artistic problems can be solved by simply taking an objective look at Aristotle's *Poetics*. The solution usually lies somewhere in that 2,000 year old handbook that might as well be called *Stories for Dummies*. Was there an equivalent solution for actors? Maybe I could find solace and craft in preparation.

Over the course of the preview process, I formulated a pre-show routine that I could trust, a series of exercises and protocol to put me in the right head space. And it was exhausting. Every, single, show, was like a hill I had to climb. And again, I didn't have a very big part, but the amount of energy I put in to each and every performance made it feel like I was performing the title role in *Hamlet*. And every night after the show I needed to spend at least a couple hours winding down from the experience. It was exhausting. At home, or rather back at my apartment, after each show I was a mix of hyper-wired and spent. I would stay up and watch mindless TV, AMC old-timey movies or cable news till two in the morning. I would consume full meals, usually an entire frozen pizza I picked up at the Jewel Marketplace that sat kitty-corner to my apartment complex. I literally gained ten pounds doing this show. I stopped watching my diet and didn't care about my health.

Every morning I would sleep in till ten, something I hadn't done in decades. Raising a child transitioned me to an early riser and I hadn't gone back since. As a writer, seven to eleven in the morning are golden hours for me, the time of the day when I get my best work done. Now I was back in my 20s and 30s, when late night adventures were a regular part of my life, going to bed late, waking up late. This was different, though. This was not fun and games. It was survival. I needed sleep, because without it my mind was mush.

So was "a routine" the solution to my anticipated stage fright? No. At least I don't think so. Probably it made things better, because I did make it through all the previews so far,[13] but who

---

13. Steppenwolf has two weeks of previews. On Broadway these performance-rehearsals go on for a month or more. At the average regional theatre in the U.S,. there are usually no more the three or four.

knows? Because I never wavered from the routine.

The fear of going up on lines continued.

And I sure as hell was not having fun. And for the first time I started having regrets. This was supposed to be an adventure. Thinking back a couple months, I remembered I had many friends who encouraged me to go back on stage. In fact, I can't recall any who didn't. They thought it would be a great way to shake things up artistically, get outside my comfort zone, and honestly, I thought so too. But here I was, that much closer to opening night, and looking ahead at nearly 50-plus performances and I was absolutely, positively miserable.

Acting felt strange and unfamiliar. Years ago, I remembered it as a rush, a rewarding and sometimes out of body experience that took me to places in my mind I'd never been. A cosmic event of connecting with an audience, feeling the power of oneness with them and reaching for the rare moments when everything on stage, and essentially the world, made sense.

I'm referring, of course, to my time before *The Grapes of Wrath*, before stage performance anxiety had crept into my real world. In part, I was looking forward to rediscovering that mystical experience I remembered having on stage. But it wasn't there, it wasn't happening. And to top it all off, I wasn't even experiencing that damned stage fright. This was some sort of dull, existential borderline that had me wondering what theatre was all about. I was a grown-ass man, on stage, wearing someone else's clothes and pretending to be another person. And people, strangers, were paying good money—a lot of money in some cases—to watch me (and others) pretend to be other people in a made up world. What the hell did it all mean?

One night, towards the end of previews, I'd had it. I was exhausted and wondering what I could do to change things up and get out of my perpetual funk. I missed home desperately. But I had avoided talking to Sue about my predicament. At this point, about five weeks into my stint, she was exhausted with being a single parent, and she was not looking forward to the remaining six weeks ahead. We were both miserable. I didn't want to bother her with my problems, especially when they had to do with regrets about taking this job. But I was desperate. I needed an outlet. I needed my partner, so one night after the show I told her what I was feeling.

Sue is an actress, and an accomplished one at that. She has an impressive list of film and television credits, but what she really loves and lives for—like most actors I know—is a chance to act on stage. Live performance is where it's at, where most actors feel they get to practice their craft. Once out of the rehearsal room, there's no director or writer who gets in the way. It's unlike working behind the camera. The actor gets to put out energy to an audience, which will, usually, reciprocate with a reaction and like energy. In film and television, the actor gives a performance that is handed over to a director and editor who will use this take or that, and cut it into the story they're after. They can, and will, manipulate a performance to their liking. Hell, they may even decide to cut an actor out of the film entirely. There is nothing comparable to this on stage, where the actor is in total control of his or her performance from beginning to end. They aren't the tools of the machine, they are the machine. They are the principal story tellers. And the experience is a meaningful one, filled with community and shared experience.

Or so I was told. Or remembered.

But here I was, whining about my existential crisis, asking Sue my Albert Camus questions about the meaning of theatre, relating to her my confusion on stage, and wondering why anyone ever thought it was a good idea for me to get back on the boards. Why does anybody act at all? I was in a state, I told her, devoting all my energies to remembering my lines and nothing more. I was determined not to make a fool of myself, which meant merely getting through each show. And the audience, I insisted, was only there to see me to fail, to fall on my face. I was a tight rope walker, working without a net, in front of a circus crowd waiting for me to crash to the ground to a humiliating death.

Sue listened. And when I was done, she let me have it. First, she wanted to know why I'd put myself and our family through this—three months away from home, and for what? So I could bitch and moan about an opportunity most actors would die for?

She quickly moved on to my obsession with memorization. Why the hell was I still on about that? Every single actor struggles with lines, she told me. And every actor finds a way around them. There is no doubt I was going to forget lines, words, on stage— everyone does once in a while. But it would never be that bad. It's never that bad. Well, not ever, I thought. We all have those anecdotes, don't we, when the actor crashes and burns and turns a standard issue performance into a story for the ages. Think of Bob. Think of Joe Mantegna in the premier of *Glengarry Glen Ross*.[14]

---

14. At the Goodman Theatre opening night of David Mamet's seminal play, *Glengarry Glen Ross*, Joe Mantegna, in the role of real estate conman Ricky Roma, sitting opposite Billy Petersen on a set depicting a Chinese restaurant, froze at the start of a six page monologue. As if infected by a virus, Peterson froze as well, and the two sat there in silence for what seemed like an eternity.

Sue went on, hopped up and seeing red. And then… and then, she said on something I will never forget.

"Why don't you stop worrying about your lines, and start worrying about your character?"

I was honestly too much in a state to listen to the advice and let it land in that moment, but that doesn't mean I didn't hear it, or would not recall it later.

Ultimately, that conversation was an all out argument that took both of us a couple days to recover from. But somewhere along the line, I let her advice sink in: "Why don't I stop worrying about my lines, and start thinking about my character?"

Over the last few previews, I took this to heart and started to think about Yevgeny Dorn, and how he was different from me, and in which ways we were the same. I thought about my rehearsals, how I had discovered how this guy carried himself, how he moved and spoke and related to others in his universe. I thought about his past, his backstory, his future, where he was going, his intentions with Polina, his confusion about the world around him, his faults and insecurities hiding underneath his cynical and proud exterior. He was a man without a family. Or rather, these friends were his family, and perhaps he was aware of how alone he was in the world. Dorn lived in some sort of house, a nice one I assumed—a bachelors pad?—somewhere on a lake, far from the city. He was well-off, he had no children. He went off secretly, frequently, to the continent, probably with a couple friends, probably engaging in

---

Eventually, Joe remembered a line at the end of the scene and the two moved on from there. The play proceeded without further incident, but everyone in the audience knew they had just witnessed a fuck-up for the ages. The world premiere of one of America's best plays of the twentieth century went on, but with a big chunk of its middle missing. This story is folklore in theatre circles.

multiple affairs. And though he was lonely, most likely he preferred this life to one of obligations and attachments.

I knew this guy. Because part of him was in me. Because I had done the work. And I had put it all on ice over the past week and a half in order to simply get through the show. But I didn't need to do that. In fact, I needed to do just the opposite. The whole live-before-an-audience experience had taken me out of myself and away from artistry. I knew what I had to do now—I needed to take the proverbial leap into the unknown, trust my body and my brain and actually live the part. And over the next few performances, I took that leap. And gradually I started to work my way out of my existentialist funk and back into the art of acting. The shift felt like a huge weight lifted from my shoulders.

I knew these lines. They were a part of me. I wanted to be word perfect—and mostly I was. But I gave myself permission to mess up, and I don't think there was one single show that I did not substitute a word here and there, or occasionally (but not often) drop an entire sentence. As long as I got the gist of the scene, what did it matter? Unless of course you take into consideration it might trip up my fellow actors, which it did, a couple of times over the course of the run, but no more than that. I noticed, in fact, that aside from a couple heavy hitters (or idiot savants), most everyone in the cast messed up once or twice. Words would fly from people's brains at a moment's notice. They would skip lines. A couple of times actors even missed whole entrances.

And then there was the other kind of "going up on lines," or rather a "going out to lunch" that actors occasionally experienced. The lines would be word perfect, but there was nothing going on behind the eyes, the mask. Their performance was on automatic pilot. And I learned—or rather it occurred to me—that this was worse than forgetting lines. Not being there, present and available, was the principal danger, at least of this particular production, when the success or failure depended on everyone being present for everyone else. If not, the words Chekhov wrote were dead on arrival.

So yes, the nerves gradually disappeared—not entirely, but enough for me to see the other side of despair, and lift the curtain from the real world to the artifice we were creating on stage—the world of this production of *Seagull* at Steppenwolf Theatre. Every night thereafter, I fell into this world and attempted to get lost in it. I allowed myself to feel the connection between Dorn and the other characters. And in turn, for me, the bond between the cast and the audience became stronger, show by show, week by week.

I led with character. That was the key that unlocked the door. Quite simply, before I made every entrance, I reminded myself what I wanted—subtextually, not on the surface—and how badly I wanted it. I had to leave myself out of the equation. Which is ironic, because it takes a certain amount of ego for a person to put themselves out there and be an actor in the first place. But that actor cannot succeed, cannot approach acting nirvana, unless and until that same ego is stomped out, destroyed and sublimated, surrendered to the production as a whole.

One of the lessons I remember the old guard of the S.T.C. ensemble repeating more than a few times in my early association with the company, before I joined the ensemble, was that it took all the actors on stage to pull through any given performance on any given night. If one actor was feeling off, the rest of the cast would need to pick up the slack and pull the extra weight, put forth an effort to compensate for that actor's "bad night." That actor would, in turn, be there for the others on their bad nights. One conjures an image of a team—any team. Terry Kinney used to use the '90s Michael Jordan Bulls as an example. A group of five, playing the court, playing off one another, with the healthy picking up the slack of the ill, or those off their game, while the group marches down the court towards the basket. One battle over, the next begins, with a new set of circumstances. Who's off this game? Well, let's adjust and make it happen. Stare the fear of failure in the face by leaning on others unafraid. No one gets left behind, everyone wins. Mission accomplished. We killed. We slayed… the audience.

9

Force of Habit

"It makes no small difference, then, whether we form habits of one kind or another from our very youth; it makes a very great difference, or rather all the difference."
— Aristotle, *The Nicomachean Ethics*

ROUTINE AND TRADITION have always been a key part of my life. I think because the world of theatre artists is so transient, we look for familiarity, and find that not in things, but in actions and habits. With every show, whether it be directing or writing, I try to find the rhythm of my daily life. There's a time to go to the gym, there's the place I go to get my coffee every morning at the same time, my diet, my clothes, my time away from social media, puzzles I do on the New York Times website. Director Tommy Kail, who directed two of my shows, is a creature of habit. At the start of every rehearsal period, he used to find a bodega nearby that would make him an egg sandwich exactly how he liked it, and he would go to that same bodega every morning before every rehearsal. Structure keeps one focused and, hopefully, moving in a forward direction.

My walk from my River North apartment to Steppenwolf Theatre. 2.2 miles each way.

So it was with my acting, but even more-so. The other out-of-town actors took public transportation, car, or bike to the theatre. I walked, which wasn't easy given the two-and-two-tenths mile route each way (four and a half miles round trip). The trek from apartment to theatre took at least forty-five minutes with no stops, and the exercise was as much as I'd get doing a regular workout. So I hoofed it practically every day. And when we began performances, I carved out an even more exacting routine. I would arrive at the theatre 50 minutes before curtain, park my backpack in my dressing room, sign in, head on up to one of the empty rehearsal rooms on the fourth floor, practice piano on a cheap, out of tune upright the theatre owned and rarely used. Then I would lie down and meditate for about 10 minutes. After that, I would head down to the stage for a quick warm-up with three of my fellow ensemble (always the same four in this group: Joey, Eli, Caroline, and myself). Then it was one flight up to the dressing room, change into my costume, drink an Emergen-C, brush my teeth and eat a teaspoon of honey.[15] By now, Jeff Perry would have arrived and we would run lines together.

Over the backstage intercom, we'd hear the call for places. And because Jeff had an entrance near the top of the show, he would leave the dressing room, at which time I had exactly thirteen minutes before my first entrance. I would close the door, turn down the monitor to a whisper and dim the lights. I used this time to practice my guitar and run lines over and over. I would then head down for my entrance every night at the same exact time: Nina's first entrance. Caroline Neff (Nina) ran on stage with an admirable burst of excited energy, so it wasn't hard to miss. I figured out during previews that this gave me ample time to get backstage and settle in before my entrance.

Passing what would soon be dubbed the "holding area"—a small, sound-proof room adjacent to the new theatre's backstage—I would pass Joey (Trigorin) and Karen Rodriguez (Masha). They'd ad lib something encouraging, like "Go get 'em champ" or "You got this!" And then, like a contender headed for the ring, I

---

15. A trick I stole from Joey Slotnick. He had an expensive, local honey into which he dipped and ate a spoonful before every show. I happened to be around one night when Joey was doing this, and he turned to me with a raised brow as if to say "Aren't ya gonna ask me about the honey?" Which I did, and he told me it was one of his pre-show traditions, something he started from his college days at SMU. The next day, I bought my own damn tiny 10 dollar jar of rare New Zealand honey from Trader Joe's and made this part of my routine. Was I ever in danger of losing my voice? Don't think so. Did it help? No idea. But it couldn't hurt.

would bound down the steps and through the soundproof door that separated the real world and the made-up one into the dark void of the backstage area… then through another door, past a curtain—still dark—where I would find Sandra Marquez. Our blocking had us entering together, or rather, her chasing me. Sort of. Dorn was in his own world, eager to get to "Treplev's performance of his new play." Polina was an afterthought, a dalliance whom I (Dorn) wasn't in fear of losing.

Backstage, Sandra would be waiting there in the same spot at the same time every night—her own routine. I would come around slowly, so as not to startle her, and then give her a generous hug. This became our tradition every night, established early on when I felt disconnected with Sandra, or Polina, at the start of previews. This was the period I was most at sixes and sevens about with my performance. In the end, I felt our work on stage together was terrific and connected, varied and always interesting—my take anyway. Now that I think back on it, I probably could have been more complimentary about Sandra's performance. She's a consummate actress with talent to spare, who uses every bit of it to hit a home run every night. Her work ethic is enviable.

I remember after a particularly rough night during previews, after one of our scenes, we came off stage, and I knew I'd done badly. The scene was choppy, I was in my head, not entirely there. I wondered if Sandra had noticed, and as we both headed up the stairs to our dressing rooms, she turned and asked "So, what is it you usually do, writing or directing?"

Getting back to the routine. Sandra and I would hug and that calmed me down significantly. It made me feel not so much alone.

And I started to notice everyone, not just me, actors and back stage crew, had their own, individual routines, their own same movements night after night. And this became the collective machinery of the show. Little by little we were establishing the secret, unspoken language of this beast called the Steppenwolf *Seagull*. I noticed I passed the same people at the same times in the same places night after night—little variations here and there, but practically the same. Backstage was yet another living, breathing organism, or performance, created by an ensemble of cast and crew. This realization that we were all pulling in the same direction helped in my conversion from hack actor to actor with a conscience. Even now, looking back at that part of the experience, I appreciate what I'd long ago forgotten: theatre is a mysterious practice—forged by craft—that transcends everyday interaction, and turns our lives into art.

10

The End of the Beginning

"If you want a happy ending... that depends, of course, on where you stop your story."

— Orson Welles

LONG AGO, Steppenwolf's policy was to invite reviewers to opening night, which created a stressful and strange event in which half the audience was quiet and judgmental while the other was insanely vocal and supportive. In this circumstance, no one got a true representation of what the show was really like and how it might play before an average audience. As Steppenwolf grew in stature over the years and there were many more requests to review its shows, critics were moved to the last couple previews before opening, which made for a really fun opening (because of, course, there were no critics), but created a very weird and highly judgmental atmosphere around the last couple previews. A few years ago, Steppenwolf decided to invite a few select critics to opening night, reasoning that a handful of sourpusses might be influenced in a positive way by the general enthusiasm surrounding them.

For *Seagull*, it didn't matter to me when the critics came because I stopped reading reviews ages ago. I never found them helpful, only destructive. I have a brother, Robert, who used to review theatre and for a time was on staff at Playbill.[16] He refused to believe theater artists never read reviews. He insisted it was a lie, just a way to make an actor, or director or writer, feel empowered in an arena in which they have no power. Probably he's right, at least in some cases. All the same, I really never read reviews anymore, especially when it comes to plays I've written. I'm a pretty good writer. I think. I mean, I'm not great, but I've made a career of it. I am acutely aware my plays are not particularly cool or fashionable in a theater sense. I'm a big proponent of plot. something I believe most playwrights neglect today. They focus instead on character and message. There are many reasons for this, but I think primarily, it's because television and film have co-opted plot as its own and theater artists have naturally, and perhaps subconsciously, drifted towards something that sets themselves apart from a more populist medium.

Regardless, I do not read critics. And I was under the assumption that most of the important ones would be reviewing *Seagull* on opening night.

So I was surprised when, on the preview before opening, standing backstage before my first entrance, I could sense a definite change in the energy coming from the audience. Or maybe it was listening over the intercom and hearing crickets to a couple of surefire laughs. Backstage, people were tense. I know I was.

---

16. Tired of theater and its tribal mentality, Robert, or Bobby to our family, transitioned to become a writer of spirits just as the cocktail revolution was hitting its stride. He no longer writes about theatre. He is his own boss and very happy sipping libations for a living.

Incidentally, the night before, Thursday—two nights before ope-ning—Joey coaxed me into going out for a drink after the show. I had one martini. Just one. I figured I deserved it after two weeks of white-knuckling it through previews. And it relaxed me. But later that evening I had trouble falling asleep. Maybe it was the alcohol, I don't know. I've noticed as I get older, hard liquor has adverse effects on me and getting a good night's sleep is certainly one of them. All day the next day, I was tired, sleep deprived. I felt like crap. I remember I followed through with my usual routine: the walk, the meditation, the honey, all of it. I doubled down on reciting my lines just to be sure, but none of it mattered. Just before I went on, I felt a thick tension in the air, and became acutely aware of my fatigue.

I went on stage and the rest of the show was a blur. I was elsewhere, outside myself, outside the theatre, or looking at my lines on the front of my brain, traveling alongside my performance—or lagging slightly behind it—while I slogged through the show on auto-pilot. I was anywhere but on stage and connecting with the person across from me. At one point early on, I even went up on a line. It was during my speech to Treplev in Act I. Namir, who is a supremely giving performer, stayed right there with me, engaged, completely in character. It looked like he would have waited all day for me to get back on track. Given the place in the scene, there was really nothing he could do or say anyway, it was all up to me. Eventually I found a word, latched on to it, connected it with a couple other words that formed a sentence (I think), and I found my way back into the speech. It sort of felt like I had fallen over a precipice of a cliff, somehow grabbed onto a tree branch, struggled, flailed and eventually pulled myself up onto solid ground. The rest of the scene I had down pat. Namir left the stage, as scripted, after Masha (Karin Rodriguez) made her entrance, at which point the two of us played out our brief scene. We exited and Act I came to an end. Offstage, no one mentioned my fuck up, but that didn't stop me from beating myself up. Why did I go out for a drink the night before? Never again. I forced myself to forget the whole thing and focus on getting through the rest of the play.

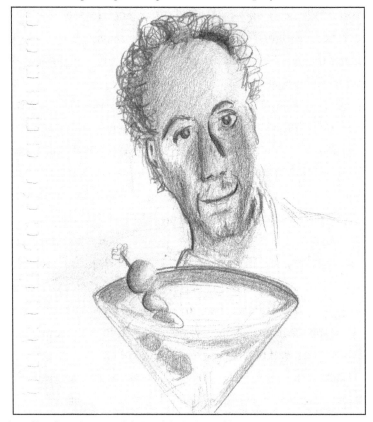

Joey Slotnik and my martini, the night before critics.

One of the better parts of getting older is understanding the value of forgetting—not as in things like forgetting one's lines on stage, of course, but in the willful forgetting of anything that's gone bad. It's a salvation, really, to be able to just pretend the bad thing that just happened never actually happened at all. It allows us to move forward, like so many ignorant and happy nitwits with no bad memories, only good ones. And at that particular point in my time and life, looking at three more acts in front of me, I needed to forget, I needed to move forward. I sucked it up and steeled myself to make the rest of the show the best it could be. And despite my little, temporary brain drain in Act I, I wasn't a disaster the rest of the night. "Worry about your character, not your lines," was my mantra, Sue's voice in my head, and my way out. And it worked. Once again.

Still, the energy coming from the audience was D.O.A. It was never my habit, or want, to look at the audience, into their eyes. Some actors can do that. Like Joey. He would come off stage some nights and say "Did you see the Covid mask on that guy in the second row on the north side of the house with the grinning Joker mouth on it? What an asshole." And I'd be like, "I have no idea what you are talking about." The audience, even when they were six inches away, was like a blur: out of focus, practically invisible.

But that night, you didn't need to see the audience to feel the energy drain. There was absolutely nothing coming from them. And on top of that, the house was only half full! All through previews Steppenwolf had been struggling to fill seats.

Back in the heyday of the company's coolness and popularity, S.R.O. houses were never a problem. The theatre was bolstered by a hefty subscription base and it was hard to get a ticket for any Steppenwolf show on any given night. But that was then, this is now. Over the course of the past decade or so, subscriptions have been in a free fall. The old model of the reliable advance-pay audience, forever the baseline for any regional theatre's operating budget, is no longer working. Today, people want more flexibility in planning their evenings out. At the height of the subscription boom, Steppenwolf had more than 25,000 subscribers. In 2022, that number had dwindled to a mere 8,000 "flex-pass" holders.

Add to this, over the years, Steppenwolf has been gradually changing its play line-up from familiar, well-known classics to more risky fare and new plays. Audiences are not as keen to take risks (my guess, not based on any hard data) especially as ticket prices go up. Play selection at Steppenwolf in particular has become increasingly narrow in its P.O.V. In the old days, Steppenwolf hits like Sam Shepard's *True West* and Lyle Kessler's *Orphans* were plays that expressed the human condition. That is to say, they made an attempt to reach the collective subconscious, to find what is common among us rather the rather than pull us apart. Today, any theatre-goer would be hard-pressed to find a new play that is not spawned from current events and social justice. Not that those plays aren't important—hell, I made my career on directing mostly agitprop theatre—but would wager to say we've lost a balance.

Another issue the theatre was contending with was no-shows. I touched on this earlier, but for a while—even before the pandemic—Steppenwolf had noticed that many people would buy tickets and then not show up for the performance. After the pandemic, this was understandable. One might buy a ticket and then decide at the last minute not to go for fear of being exposed to the lingering virus. But before? Some guessed that people bought tickets in a gesture of solidarity, with no intention of showing up in person, a sort of pat on the back and an in-kind donation to the theatre. That may be true. But what most of these kind-hearted theatre-no-goers may not understand is that half empty houses has a detrimental effect on the cast and crew. It's debilitating to play to half-empty houses.

An equally reasonable explanation for the empty seats, though—and admittedly contrary to the position I argued just two paragraphs ago—may be that people just aren't interested in seeing Chekhov. I had to ask myself, would I buy a ticket to see *Seagull* in this day and age? Probably not, when there are so many entertainment options. And in theatre, revivals of plays are on the wane. Thirty years ago, regional theatres lived off a steady diet of Williams, Miller and O'Neill. Not today.

Whatever the reason, during previews we were never at capacity. Not once. We may have been sold out on paper a few times, but that did not translate to an actual full house. So, back on that Friday night before opening: though it wasn't a surprise the house was half empty, the audience reaction made it feel like there was hardly anyone out there at all. And I was not the only one who was having an off night. Practically everyone in the cast was struggling. Connections were missed, and sometimes non-existent. People fumbled lines. One actor missed an entire entrance. Backstage, the cast walked the circular alleyways as if in a fog, wondering what we had done to deserve such a tough crowd.

Need I mention that this was the night all the A-list critics had come to review the show?

* * *

Opening night, the night after, was much better. It was an event. The show went well. We were celebrating a monumental achievement: the christening of a first class theatre in one of the world's largest (and best) metropolises. An hour before curtain, Yasen called the cast for a meeting in one of the board rooms situated on the third floor of the new theatre complex. During tech and previews, the director and the cast get sort of separated as a result of the tight schedule and the many things going on that have nothing to do with acting or performance. Yasen wanted us to all be together one last time before we embarked on our run. The cast gathered round an enormous table and we took in the moment. A lot of kind words were said (despite the disastrous performance from the night before). We celebrated the work so far. I made sure to give a shout out to Jeff Perry for his dedication to the new theatre and Steppenwolf in general, from the day he helped found it. Jeff was his usual self, and a little emotional as he reminded us that "ensemble" was what it was all about. Sandra spoke eloquently about this being her first chance to perform after two years of pandemic isolation. I had forgotten this was the case. Everyone in that room was having their first live performance after two and a half years off the stage. Some tears were shed that night, around that enormous table.

And then we went back to work.

I barely recall the show. It went well, no flubbed lines. The audience was definitely on our side, but there were still empty seats! This was the only downside that night. I think everyone felt pretty good, but damn, those empty seats put a damper on things. This was the opening of a multi-million dollar, brand new theatre, 10 years in the making, a once in a generation event for the city. Later, we would find out—as was the case on many other nights during the run—that the house had been way oversold and the empty seats were a result of no-shows. Booooo!

✳ ✳ ✳

Post performance I went out into the crowd—grabbed a glass of wine—moved towards the reception, not embarrassed. My performance was respectable, I decided. Not brilliant, but definitely not bad for a writer/director. I was disappointed to discover a lot of the friends I'd expected to be there that night had left the reception early. The ones who had stayed didn't offer much comfort. And this, I learned was going to be the start of another performance anxiety issue I would have to endure for the next seven weeks: the phenomenon known as the Ungrateful Theatre-goer.

Now, I'm not of the mind that anyone who sees a show and hates it needs to lie about it (though lying is certainly a fair option). But I do believe that, if a person insists on being absolutely truthful, then they need to go all the way and not deflect. In other words, if you insist on staying after my show to see me, and then not say anything about that show or my performance in it, or you choose to engage in any sort of other insensitive and rude behavior, you are a dick.

Here is a list of the kinds of post-show dicks:

The Literalist. The person that parrots the zinger we've all heard "It looked like you were having fun up there!" or "You should have seen yourself!" Any actor who hears these words will, of course, reflexively wait for the follow-up phrase or word that might inform them the viewer actually liked the show. Alas, it will never come. And the worst part of the Literalist is these are generally, primarily people in the business who know better.

The Ignoramus. These are people not used to going to theatre and definitely not used to seeing performers after a show. They simply forget to say anything kind, or don't know the performer is in a vulnerable place. Instead, The Ignoramus stands there and chats about traffic on the way to the theatre or where they ate before the show. Forgive them, Lord, for they know not what they do.

The Deflector. The theatre-goer who will talk about everything in the show they loved and hated except your performance. The Deflector is kinder than most post-show dicks, able to give off a generally positive and enthusiastic response because, more often than not, they have trod the boards themselves and know the damage a bad word will do. But they're still dicks.

The Magician. This is the friend or colleague who saw the show—and you know they saw the show—but they did not stay after to say hi or offer props. Then you see them a few days later and they act as if the show never happened and they were never there. They have, in effect, made the show *disappear*.

The Equivocator. The friend who suggests your performance was bad but it's not your fault. "You're brilliant, but this production failed you miserably." The Equivocator is more often than not motivated by jealously.

On opening night, most of my friends in attendance were experienced theatre-goers. My sister, Britta, a real estate agent living in Naperville, and brother-in-law Dennis, were not. They had found a table in the corner of the Front Bar—the restaurant attached to the Steppenwolf's lobby—and I took refuge there while I nursed a wine and, out of the corner of my eye, searched for friendly friends I could count on. Britta and Dennis were happy to talk about getting to the reception table before anyone else, and about how Dennis was able to sneak into the show without being vaccinated. Eventually one of my friends found me: Dale Buck, a Steppenwolf supporter and co-sponsor of my last directing/writing effort at Steppenwolf *Lindiwe*. Dale, a loyal friend, always had a good word to say and a smile on his face, and I was elated to see him… till I realized he had, that night, turned into a Deflector, eager to talk about everything except the show and me on stage as an actor. Or perhaps he was a little bit Ignoramus, not privy to the pusillanimous insecurities of the actor. Either way, he was pissing me off, so I wriggled my way out of that conversation and reinserted myself into the rapidly dissipating crowd.

Key art!

I can usually tell if a show is going to be a hit or a dud simply by how rapidly the post-opening party dissipates. Here, people were headed for the exits pretty quickly. I ran into Laura Crosby, an old friend and my former Chicago acting agent. We hugged. She was warm and friendly, but once again, did not say one thing about the show or my performance in it. Another Deflector? We talked about the new theater and how and when we might get together while I was in town, but I wasn't in the mood. I reached for another glass from a passing cater-waiter and moved on. I talked to a few others who (at long last) were complimentary. But by then my mood had grown dark. I missed my family and was feeling the effects of one too many drinks. After an hour or so I said bye to Britta and Dennis, who were on their second helping from the buffet table, and took an Uber back to my apartment. I peeled off my suit and, before I went to bed, looked at the production calendar I had taped to the corporate wall of my corporate apartment in my corporate building. I stood there, a little drunk, staring at the white squares that made up May and June. The show had opened. I went on stage and did my part. The ghost of *The Grapes of Wrath* had been exorcised and put to rest. The fear I'd encountered the last time I tread the boards had disappeared. Vanished. I did it.

Now all that was required of me was 39 more performances.

11

---·⊖⋘⊙·---

The Road to Mecca

*"There's no such thing as Perfection. But in striving for
perfection, we can achieve excellence."*

— Vince Lombardi

I SHOULD MENTION HERE—it's as good a place as
any—that all through previews, Yasen could not have been a better
advocate for the cast and production. He was always ebullient,
effusive with his belief in us and the show. He had us believing
we were doing something very special that could reach the best of
what Steppenwolf had to offer.

I had my doubts. Was anyone else really feeling this? Thinking
back, during *Grapes*, I never felt we were that great, and *every-
fucking-body* loved that show. So what did I know? And what did
it matter anyway? Whatever I was thinking or believing at this
point, Yasen's enthusiasm was not for nothing. As in rehearsals,
Yasen continued to protect us with his belief and faith in us. As
an actor, he must have known the precarious cliff we were approaching when bringing into the mix that essential last phase of any
production process: the audience. Yasen, I am certain, knew,

instinctively or by experience (or both), that if nothing else, the captain of this ship needed to let us know from time to time that we were on the right course. And also, that he would not want to sail with any other crew.

He not only told us, but wrote to us, sending us missives, e-mailed daily the morning after each preview, gently guiding us through this uncertain period. This is one example which came to us after the third performance:

Morning thoughts on Seagull.

'Yes, I'm getting more and more convinced that it's not about new or old forms, but what you write, without thinking of any forms, what comes pouring freely out of your heart' Konstantin, Seagull Act IV. It is the greatest advice that you can give to any artist and simply replace the word write with perform, play or paint. The genius of Chekhov lies precisely in his simplicity, and any lack of pretension that gets in the way of the bond that the artist establishes with the public. As I mentioned early in our rehearsal process the biggest challenge in performing Chekhov's work is to stay simple, clear and focused on the immediate objective. In my many performances as an actor of his characters I have always found this to be the most difficult task. To completely delete any knowledge of what is about to happen, or what you did the night before and you felt so good about it and to stay clear-eyed and focused on the person you're talking to and feel the actual need to say the words as if they are coming out of your mouth for the first time. It is one of the first things we learn in drama school and it is always the most challenging to execute with absolute faith and naiveté. In Chekhov's world it is absolutely

necessary to have this kind of immersion, concentration and focus. The world of his characters is built on the fact that you the actor is enough. He fought against all gimmicks, actor tricks, prat falls and contrived behavior that takes the audience out of the world they have been invited to be part of. When Stanislavsky would ask him about clarification on practically anything Chekhov would simply reply "Listen, it's all written in there." To me this is an invitation to trust Chekhov's words.

Since the audience entered our world, I have been noticing the element of performance slowly creep in the production. Of course, it's natural, I understand. We're not doing this only for ourselves, the audience is part of our world even more so in this theatre being surrounded by it. Their energy influences our energy, their behavior has an impact on our behavior. However, we need to remember that we're not there to please them. We need to stay honest and not give in to the temptation to impress them. Last night I felt there was a lot of muscle and "performance" in some of your scenes. There are of course the objective factors such as nerves, fatigue and the nature of repetition. My only advice is again, trust the text, trust Chekhov, trust the work you have done over the last 5 weeks in the rehearsal room. Each one of you has crafted beautiful, complicated, three-dimensional characters that are relatable, funny and heart breaking at the same time. The audience should not have the feeling that they are watching a performance but rather that they have been accidentally dropped in the midst of this group of people, many having their existential crisis only a few feet away from them completely unaware that they are being watched. I know, I know it is easier said than done but I want to repeat again you are enough and trust the text. Any unnecessary internal pauses, interruptions, comments on your-

self and other characters through snickering and tonal inflections that only take away the focus away from the story of your character and bring attention to you the actor performing a memorized text.

The show is very strong and in great shape. Even in its current shape last night I received several really enthusiastic responses from a few Eastern European audience members including an elderly Russian couple who were so visibly moved and affected by the production and your performances that I started doubting myself whether I am overly critical and demanding. But then, they haven't seen what I have seen during our 5 weeks of rehearsals. Yes, we have a good show. But having seen what I have seen, I don't think that's good enough. We have the potential of having an extraordinary show, a theatrical event to baptize our new theatre. An opportunity to create another glorious chapter in the history of our beloved Steppenwolf to take its place among True West, Balm in Gilead, Time of Your Life and August: Osage County. And we're very close. You just need to let it pour feely out of your heart."

Yasen's prodding, enthusiasm, and constant care had the desired effect. Over the next few weeks I could feel the production getting richer and more grounded as we went along. And perhaps it wasn't only the notes that got us there, but they sure as hell didn't hurt.

I stopped directing theater on a steady basis when I started to get more lucrative work writing for television. I also kept up with my directing of operas, which happens to pay more. And opera is more fun for the director because the canvas of the production design is so much larger and well-funded. Directing theatre—aside from directing my own plays—had, sadly, become a chore in which

I thought—and felt increasing over the years—I was meant to be more of a group therapist than anything else. To coax a good performance from an actor, I needed to access each individual and test them for their strengths and weakness. Some actors are needy and require constant attention. Others want to be left alone and given space to go through their own process. Some are novices of the craft and demand instruction, while others are old hands who rely on bags of tricks they hold on to and are stubborn to give up. Creating an ensemble requires a certain amount of expertise in wrangling the proverbial cats. After directing, oh say, over 50 plays over the years, I'd grown weary of the task. No, that's not entirely true. To this day I know I have the talent to direct plays, I just may have lost patience. Yasen had/has patience to spare. And passion. These letters prove it. And as he wrote them — and I read them and tried to implement them—I decided that in any future directing projects—theatre or otherwise—I would need to follow his example. I used to write cast notes like this. Little love letters that were, you hoped, like fertilizer dusting the ground, nourishing the roots, that would help grow the production. I remember past shows for which I would give an impassioned speech before every performance. And I would invariably get immediate results. The troops, my actors, would rally to the cause and take on the (prospective) hostile audience, winning them over, planting the victory flag. I remember writing notes to actors and passing them backstage via the stage manager before a show, and then see the effects of my words play out on stage and bring a show one step closer to the perfection we all strove for.

Somewhere along the line—perhaps around the time I moved to L.A. and my interest in television and film took root—I stopped writing those letters. I stopped giving those speeches. I was still working, but the work was not as rewarding as it had been in the past. I thought maybe this was a result of fatigue or over-confidence. The results were good, at least decent, but my heart was not entirely into it. And this produced a finished product that was less than what it could have been. Or should have been. And it left me feeling empty artistically.

Yasen Peyankov has a big heart. He lives in Chicago and teaches theatre at the University of Illinois in Chicago. He was born and raised in Bulgaria before he came to the United States and settled in Chicago, where he started a storefront company, The European Repertory Company, a group of artists devoted to revivals of European, and some contemporary plays, rehearsed over extended weeks in the European fashion. I never saw one of their productions (I had left Chicago by then for parts west) but by all reports, they did good work. Good enough, certainly, for Yasen to get noticed by Steppenwolf and Ensemble Member Tina Landau, who cast him in back to back productions of *Time to Burn* and *Berlin Circle.* He fit in well with the company and, a few years later, was invited in.

Did I mention Yasen adores Chekhov? By 2021 he had staged all his plays except one: *Seagull.* His passion for the play and doing it right was clear from the start. But just because the play had opened didn't mean he was finished. When I direct plays, it's usually an out of town engagement. Most non-theatre folks assume the director attends every performance of a run. Not so. It's an understandable misconception, but professional directors are usually off to their next gig the day after a show opens, in another city far away. But that's not the only reason directors sometimes never, or rarely, return to see their shows. I, for one, have a tough time revisiting all the mistakes I can no longer fix. Or I might see wrong choices I made that are baked into the production and cannot be reversed. And the audience--it changes nightly. This is at once a curse and the saving grace of theatre. There can be wildly different reactions from audiences watching plays. This demonstrates the aliveness and immediacy of theatre. It's also unnerving to witness as director, because things that worked one night fail the next. And you can never put your finger on exactly why. Returning to a show might mean encountering a hostile audience that spews venom and changes your mind about a show you thought was actually okay.

So when I leave a show the day after it opens, I'm generally happy I have the excuse of distance not to return. I prefer looking at performance reports, the stripped down, factual communique compiled and sent out by e-mail from the stage manager after every performance. These little missives give the house count: "348 out of 500 on a Tuesday"—not bad, audience reaction: "A few standees." Okay. I'll take it." Any odd events or audience and actor peccadilloes: "Woman exited the theatre mid second act mumbling 'This is bullshit!" What? Fucking asshole.

Things like that. I can glean a lot from a little, and just as much as I need to go about the rest of my day. And hey, my focus is already on the next project anyway.

But Yasen never left us. Well, first of all, he couldn't. He lives in Chicago. It would be difficult for him not to show up from time to time. But I think he loved returning to see the show, and I appreciate that about him. I remember as an actor, oh so long ago, I had felt differently. Most of the time I never liked having the director or playwright around after opening. It made me nervous, and anyway, by then it was our show, the actor's, the ensemble's, not the director's or playwright's. They had done their jobs, so be well, fuck off.

I never got this feeling with Yasen, though. His coming back to the show was like getting a visit from Grandpa. He wasn't there to judge or scold, but to check in and cheerlead. Grandpa was there with a smile and a pat on the back as he squeezed a five dollar bill into your hand when no one was looking. I liked it when I knew he was in the audience watching. And he made it clear that just because we had opened, it didn't mean our job building this show had finished. The Steppenwolf *Seagull* was a work in progress.

As it turned out, he was absolutely right. At opening, we really had just begun. We were only half-baked. Regarding my performance alone, I had just weaned myself off my lines and was merely "getting through" every performance. What was that? Was that art? Hardly.

Yasen came to see us at least once a week, and so did his assistant, Tina El Gamal, who had been a positive force in rehearsals and was now proving to be an insightful and smart proxy when Yasen was not available.

I continued with my pre-show routine, and again, the nerves never really left me. Every show was a challenge just to set foot on stage. But now, once I got there, I felt the fear fall away. As I relaxed into the show and received positive reinforcement from Yasen and Tina, I allowed myself to play, to let the scenes come to me and respond in kind, in a spontaneous and, I hoped, authentic way. Easy to say, yes, but I learned through my trial by fire that it's usually the first thing that goes out the window when I'm on stage and petrified.

I felt my fellow actors were doing the same, relaxing into the show, their characters, and their performances. There was a trust built into this ensemble, due in large part to the foundation built in rehearsals, and I felt buoyed by it. I made mistakes, yes. I flubbed a line here and there, checked out of a scene every now and again, but it didn't seem to matter, or bother the other actors. All was forgiven (or so it seemed to me) moments after any little fuck up, as long as I jumped back into the scene and recommitted. It was like being on a very aggressive dance floor and occasionally getting bumped onto the sidelines. I guess you could give up, check out and have some punch, or you could jump on the floor and get back into the action. Other actors screwed up too, got bumped and they, like I, took the hit, got back on the floor and kept dancing. We were all in the moment, in our characters and outside of them at the same time. In fact, whenever anyone screwed up on stage, it was pretty much verboten off stage to discuss the gaff. To survive... we must all forgive, forget, and move on. This is oftentimes the secret to any marriage, isn't it? Forgive, forget and move on. There was no past, no future, only now.

I remember discussing this with Joey Slotnik about three weeks into the run (over a martini after a show—*on a night before a day off*), and I asked him "Am I ever gonna get to that one show where everything goes right?" He didn't hesitate. "No," he said, "that will never happen. And that is the joy of acting. The trying to get to that one perfect performance."

At that point he took a sip of his martini, and his thoughts went inward, and then he said:

"Yup. That will never happen."

* * *

The more we performed the show, the more comfortable I felt. And that comfort, and perhaps confidence, was soon followed by a kind of post show euphoria. I started to experience, here and there, actual discovery. These moments were real and genuine, and finding them in front of an audience of strangers, they made me feel a little like a magician performing a trick. There was a "See what I did there just now?" kind of satisfaction that had something to do with finding a true moment in life that we, the actors, and them, the audience, all agreed upon. A shared experience that brought us together and proved we were in sync, one and the same. In large part, I think these moments were times when I felt I had taken the stage, that I was comfortable in my skin and had somehow harnessed the energy needed to command the attention of the audience. I remembered these feelings from way back in my acting days, those moments when it seemed time stood still, that the audience was watching and waiting and part of the conversation.

A big part of this was me feeling a certain amount of accomplishment in molding this performance of Dorn. And I can't deny I felt a sense of pride in simply getting through the show. That was a big deal for me. That others seemed to respect what I was doing meant a lot. I was a part of this. It was the feeling you get when you're picked last for the kick ball team, but then turn out to be a minor, yet essential, part of the team's win. And because our rehearsals and the direction set by Yasen were so focused on creating the most loving and spontaneous performance, I, and the others I suspect, felt free to explore, to make things keenly spontaneous. I never planned anything, but while on stage, a thought might occur that lied outside the confines of the written script, or what we had rehearsed and the decisions I made for Dorn. And I would act on that impulse. I would get explosive on one line that was normally whispered—an adjustment that your average audience member would never detect, but my scene partner sure would. And they would react in kind. Their performance would adjust to what I had just given them. And this had a domino effect, until we would get to the next beat or agreed upon section of the scene or act, at which point we would reset, because there's no benefit in letting one little adjustment take the entire show off the tracks. In the end, despite the embellishments, we always, essentially, performed the play the way we rehearsed it.

It was an experience that not only freed me from the yoke of fears that had ensnared me early on, but allowed me to rediscover the joy I once had for acting. Or maybe I never had that and now I was discovering it for the first time. Regardless, I now understood what it was like to be an actor and want to be an actor. To have that urge to get out on stage and "pretend to be someone else". Before *Seagull*, I guess I had been looking at acting from the 30,000 foot viewpoint. But here, down on Earth, on stage in Chicago—in the moment with that trusting fellow actor across from me, capturing something the audience so wanted to experience and *believe* in—I finally got it.

Nearing the end of the run, my ideas about acting, and Steppenwolf, my artistic home, changed. Returning to the stage wasn't me simply feeding my ego. What I felt could be mostly summed up in what I experienced every evening at curtain call. Here, there was mutual appreciation between performer and audience. Especially in these days right after the pandemic, when audiences were kept away from theatre and the communal experience of large gatherings. Here, after so many months, actors were saying thank you to the folks who came out, showed up and entrusted us with this sermon called *Seagull.*

And that got me to thinking about the very first Steppenwolf productiom I saw: Caryl Churchill's *Cloud Nine.* I had just arrived in the city, dirt poor. I was living above the B.L.U.E.S. Bar on Halsted (now defunct) on the third floor with two strangers/roommates I met through the Chicago Reader. Every night I would fall asleep to the thumping baseline and Big Time Sarah singing 'Sweet Home Chicago.' On nights I wasn't working a minimum wage job, I would volunteer to usher to see theatre for free.

I remember very little about that production of *Cloud Nine*—it was so long ago and ultimately a good, but not great, play. But I do remember acting moments here and there. The Steppenwolfers taking stage, though not one of them shining any more than another. They were all equally good. And I got it. I got the ensemble thing everyone was talking about. The collective acting that mattered more to the general result than anything else. But the thing I remember most about that evening was the final bow, when Jeff Perry, Fran Guinan, Terry Kinney, Laurie Metcalf, Alan Wilder, Rondi Reed, and Joan Allen all came out on stage, as one, to show their appreciation. Despite the small, longish space (converted, apparently, from a bowling alley) the actors bowed three ways: to house left, then house right, then house center. They were first upright, then bent at the waist, with reverence—no sloppy bows here (what you might expect from a bunch known for their rock-n-roll attitude). Just pure respect and gratitude. Who knows, maybe, probably, after the show they went back to their dressing rooms and ragged on the audience for being capricious assholes, just like we did occasionally after performances of *Seagull*. It's a release.

But still, that bow is what I remember. And I sort of remember we did the same thing at the curtain call of *The Grapes of Wrath*. And now I was experiencing it again, here, acting in *Seagull*. Or *understanding* it finally. But man, did it take a long time to get there.

12

Going Home

*"I think we are well advised to keep on nodding terms
with the people we used to be, whether we find them
attractive company or not. Otherwise they turn up unan-
nounced and surprise us, come hammering on the mind's
door at 4 a.m. of a bad night and demand to know who
deserted them, who betrayed them, who is going to make
amends."*

—Joan Didion, *Slouching Towards Bethlehem*

YASEN NEVER WASTED an opportunity to come back
stage and tell us how the show was continuing to blossom and
grow and surprise him. And I think most of us actually belie-
ved him, though we weren't as enthusiastic as he. Hell, we were
in the middle of a long march towards closing night. It wasn't
time to celebrate. But it was nice to hear, even as the feeling crept
in that we'd missed our chance to make the play as good as it
could have been by opening night. Were the reviews effecting our
less-than-impressive attendance? Were the critics influencing our
audiences?

I tried not to think about that at the time, when we were in the thick of it. Yet, six months after the closing, curiosity got the best of me and I decided to take a look. I was back to my day job, writing and directing, with no acting opportunities on the horizon (or even desired). By then, I was so far removed from the show that any bad notice would have had no effect. By then, performing Dorn seemed like something I had dreamt.

And lo and behold, the reviews, on the whole, were excellent. The Chicago Daily Herald gave us three-and-a-half out of four stars.

> *"The first act of Steppenwolf's 'Seagull' is standard Steppenwolf. Robust and practiced, it is a solid piece of theatre by director Yasen Peyankov, who translated and adapted Anton Chekhov's 1896 tragicomedy to Steppenwolf's stage. And an impressive stage it is. This production—which includes longtime members Jeff Perry and Eric Simonson with recent additions Sandra Marquez, Caroline Neff and Namir Smallwood—inaugurates the company's in-the-round Ensemble Theatre.*

Four stars (out of four) from the Sun-Times:

> *"Steppenwolf ensemble member Yasen Peyankov has been working on his adaptation of Chekhov's 'Seagull' since 2008. As the opener of the new 400-seat theater in the $53 million Liz and Eric Lefkofsky Arts and Education Center, it's been in the works since pre-COVID days. When the long-gestating production finally opened over the weekend*

one thing was clear: The wait was worth it."
And of Dorn:

*"Simonson brings a predatory edge to a small-town OB/
GYN who prides himself on being 'honest' in not acting on
his attraction to the women he examines."*

Predatory edge, eh? Another reviewer thought otherwise.

*"Eric Simonson creates a gentle, likable, sincerely caring
Dr. Dorn, the only character offering support and comfort
to everyone else, even beyond his medical skills."*

So which is it? I like that—two conflicting impressions of the same character. And neither wrong.

While a couple (literally two out of the dozen critics who reviewed the show) weren't so hot on the production, every single one raved about the space. As well they should have. I cannot attest to how it was watching a play, but being on that stage was awesome. Stepping out on the boards felt like having your arms wrapped around you by the audience. It was entirely inviting and comfortable, despite any nerves I had.

So if the notices were so great, why the tepid ticket sales? And what of our no-shows? And the single ticket drought?

It's a mystery. Blame it on Covid-19, blame it on dead-white-man-writer Chekhov, blame it on the new world order facing us on the other side of the pandemic, Netflix and politics. Theatre was slow to come back. My prediction is that eventually it will be back. Decades of robust theater in the day and age of movies and television have proven over and over that people are social beings, eager to escape solitary lives and come together from time to time. But who knows. I was good friends with the late Bernie Sahlins, whom I mentioned earlier. He was a Chicago theater stalwart, producer, director, and writer. Bernie was one of the founders of The Second City, and he and his wife Jane started the Chicago International Theatre Festival, which was a brilliant and audacious, if short lived, effort to bring theatre from all over the world to Chicago. Bernie was a perennial cynic, but he loved theatre and saw everything there was to see. He had his hand in so many Chicago theatre pots it was hard to ignore him. Ironically, one repeating refrain he liked to espouse was that people don't really *need* theater, and they could do very well without it, thank you very much. And in fact, in the history of mankind, he would say, theatre has only enjoyed three brief periods of popularity: Ancient Greece (Euripides, Sophocles), Elizabethan England (Shakespeare, Marlowe), and during the twentieth century in so called "developed" countries (Shaw, Brecht, O'Neill). It's no surprise, and not even sad, that theater should die away again sometime, as it did during the dark ages, or, ostensibly, between Shakespeare's death and Shaw's heyday. And the death of theater isn't the worst thing that could happen in the world. Climate change may be, or the end of democracy, but the death of theatre? Not really.

Today, maybe a lot of folks might agree with Bernie that theater is at death's door. And probably it takes a combo platter of world pandemic and social upheaval to shake things up, for better or worse, to move the needle a little closer Theater Hospice.

One thing, though, I'm confident will never go away: story-telling. Which is primal and essential and as old as the beginning of language. It's how human beings learn, by example, telling stories of successes and failures. It's how we collectively grieve or celebrate, on hearing, together, the passage or transformation or ethical or evil individuals that become a part of our collective subconscious. Story-telling is how we survive. It's part of our DNA. Just ask Carl Jung, who theorized as much in oh so many books and scientific/spiritual treatises. From the time humans gathered together, we have dipped into one another's imaginations and seen the same beginning middle, and end worked out, if not acted out, certainly in our heads, definitely at the front of our collective brains. This, I'm confident, will never disappear. But what form it will take, who knows? Maybe it won't be in the bailiwick of American regional theatres, or Broadway. Maybe it will just be some guy sitting around that proverbial campfire telling a ghost story, or the occasional raconteur acting out a shaggy dog story in a bar. Or maybe it will be an A.I. software that has learned just the right emotional brainwave to tickle in order to get our attention. Time will tell. There are so many things in the world today that are changing so fast.

What won't change? Fear. Illusion. Courage. Risk. Imagination. Relief. All these played a part in my Indiana Dorn journey from Man-Watching-From-the-Wings to Man-Center-Stage.

✳ ✳ ✳

Sue and Henry, who skipped opening, flew out for closing weekend instead. This was one last hurdle I needed to get over. Performing for friends and strangers is one thing, but family? Your forever love and teenage son? Entirely another.

But as it turned out, it wasn't all that bad. By that time I had 55 shows under my belt. I had gone through my existential what-the-hell-is-theatre-anyway crisis and come through on the other side finding salvation in my fellow actors. I had discovered the key to overcoming my stage fright—be in the moment, dammit, no matter what. On the night they saw me, I performed my usual show. And afterwards they were supportive and complimentary. They fit in none of my post-show bad-audience categories, by the way. And actually, I think their praise was genuine. They even complimented my singing.

After the last show, the cast went out to Vinci's, a restaurant down the street from the theatre, where Jeff Perry had secured a private room, and we all had dinner and non-stop refills of wine. We made many toasts about how great we were and how awesome the show was and how much we loved and appreciated one another and what great time we had and how lucky we were. And then we parted ways.

And a week later three-quarters of the group came down with Covid-19.

Not me, fortunately. Nor Henry and Sue. No one got very sick, thankfully, but still, on an e-mail chain we all marveled that not one person in the cast had come down with Covid-19 during the entire course of the run.

I remember arriving home after three months in Chicago and taking a deep breath. I felt grateful for all I had—a nice home, my family, our dog Pippen, all my familiar things around me. I have felt this mix of nostalgia many times before, because I'm often returning home after weeks away. But never had I felt it as strongly as I did then. My great experiment returning to the stage had been an adventure. And like most adventures, there were good times and bad, highs and lows. And during the bad times, it felt like things would never, ever be good again. And in the end, after all was said and done, there was one big, overwhelming feeling of relief.

Oh, and one more thing: months after we closed—even today—I can recite my lines backwards and forwards. Somewhere along the way, those words became a part of me. I can rattle them off the tip of my tongue without even thinking.

Strange.

The cast of Steppenwolf's Seagull: From left to right: Keith Kupferer, Jon Hudson Odom, Namir Smallwood, Sandra Marquez, Elijah Newman, Karen Rodriguez, Caroline Neff, me, Luisa Strus, Joey Slotnick, Jeff Perry.

✳ ✳ ✳

How can I use all that I learned in all that I will do in the future? *Will* I use anything I learned? I know I'll certainly be thinking of my future casts of actors in a new and different light. If I'm directing, I will try to apply all the good parts of what I learned from Yasen. I know, also, I will be thinking of the actors backstage and perhaps be more aware of their journey from first rehearsal to two weeks into a run. Because I live out of town from most of the places I direct, I'm gone after opening night. It's been a long time since I was able to return and visit my productions. Which is a shame, because I know that part of Yasen's process was essential to us getting to where we needed to be. The folks who saw us early in the run certainly missed out on something special. I don't know if I will ever be able to change my work schedule, but I do have a new appreciation for the degrees to which a show grows over the course of a run.

As I writer, I hope I can take advantage of all Chekhov taught me while inhabiting one of his characters. Who knows, maybe I will improve. You can only hope (I always do). The thing about Chekhov, and what makes him such a challenge—and also such a great dramatist at the same time—is that his characters talk and think in those damned non-sequiturs. They easily abandon one train of thought for another. Though this is admirably much like real life, it's difficult to act, and, for a playwright, even harder to defend. Chekhov was only able to do this with the unwavering support of his directors Konstanin Stanislavsky and Vladimir Danchenko backing him up. I can imagine scenarios in which I have actors, directors, or dramaturges demanding I defend a certain line. "But why does he say that here? Why now, in the middle of a thought? It doesn't make any sense!" To which I might reply "Well, that's the way people behave!" I don't think that argument would go over too well. Martin McDonough, the famous playwright and Oscar-winning director, could maybe get away with it. I have a reliable source who tells me he comes to first rehearsal with the final draft of his play and refuses to change one word thereafter. More power to him.

Epilogue

"As nearly as possible in the spirit of Matthew Salinger, age one, urging a luncheon companion to accept a cool lima bean, I urge my editor… to accept this pretty skimpy-looking book."

—J.D. Salinger, *Franny and Zooey*

WEEKS, AND THEN MONTHS, after we closed, I would mention, now and again, to friends or even strangers, that I went back on the boards after three decades. Just before and while I was doing the show, however, I barely said anything to anyone about my engagement. I was afraid they would actually come and see me when my plan was to remain invisible while I tried out my experiment pretending to be an actor. So I kept as low a profile as possible. I was that nervous. On telling people after the fact, safe now—as I related in the preface of this book—eyes would light up.

One of these people was Keith Nobbs, an actor who was in my plays *Lombardi* and *Bronx Bombers*. Keith is small in stature, but what he loses in size he makes up for with pluck and charm. Thin, wiry and agile, he's capable of deep and layered emotions, oftentimes delivered with an impish grin that gets chummy laughs and adoration from audiences. He is ever present on stage and cares deeply about his craft. You never have to worry when you cast Keith Nobbs. He gets the job done. At least that's how I remembered him the second to last time I saw him, at the closing of my play *Bronx Bombers* on Broadway in 2014. Keith played the mercurial Yankee Billy Martin, and he tore up the stage in a pivotal scene opposite Francois Battiste, who played Reggie Jackson. It was really brilliant work and the kind I had come to expect and admire from Keith.

Keith and I live on opposite sides of the country—he in New York, I in Los Angeles—so, outside of work we don't see each other very much. And though I consider him a close friend, we don't keep in touch. So I was surprised when I heard in and around 2016 that Keith had suddenly given up acting. He had suffered a crisis of confidence, or rather of faith, in his craft, and his ability to deliver an honest performance. But more than that, he had come to question his motives for being an actor, and wondered if his ambitions were misguided. So he decided to go back to college and earn a degree, which he never had—a sacrifice he made when his career took off at age 18. He wanted to devote himself to something less self-serving and more secure. And apparently, Keith is a pretty smart guy, because he applied to all the top schools across the country, including Harvard, Princeton, and Yale, and got accepted to all of them. He eventually chose Stanford, which enticed him with free tuition, housing and living expenses. Not bad. Perhaps Keith was in the wrong profession after all.

For the next several years, Keith applied himself to social

anthropology and he astounded. He amazed. He went to England as part of a special research project and studied with Paulla Ebron, a specialist in his chosen field. And when he got his degree, he was offered more tuition-free opportunities to continue his studies. And did Keith accept these offers? Did he continue on this road of opportunity and academic distinction?

No, he did not. He returned to New York and picked up where he left off: acting.

Or pursuing acting. Because to act, one needs to get cast, and to get cast, one needs to audition. Unless you're the occasional A-list, or high B-list actor, it's still the only way to get a job. Or, I guess, unless you're a member of an acting company that needs your performing services in a pinch because they're opening a multi-million dollar theatre and require as much ensemble participation as possible. At any rate, auditioning is the usual way, even if you're as talented as Keith, who didn't make things easy for himself by jump-starting his revival in the middle of a pandemic. It wasn't easy, but he stuck it out, or rather, he's still sticking it out. Social anthropology is a distant memory, an adventure he experienced and is now happy to have left behind.

I reunited by chance with Keith in 2021. A group of us from *Bronx Bombers* arranged to meet at a Midtown Manhattan bar to raise a glass to actor Peter Scolari, who was also in *Bronx Bombers*, and who had recently succumbed to cancer the week before. This was when I learned all about Keith's time away from the limelight. In a style of spontaneous storytelling I had come to expect from Keith, he regaled the group with his adventures in higher education the past few years. Keith hadn't changed. He was still the same high spirited guy, eager to engage. And I wondered how he ever thought it would be a good idea to leave the stage. If there was ever a born actor, it was Keith.

After our little get together, I went about my life. I worked a few jobs, including *Seagull*, and then returned home and started writing this (ahem) memoir. And I thought about Keith—completely different story, but also someone who had acted and then left the stage and was now returning. I wondered what he might think about my little adventure, so I called to catch up.

I caught him at his parents home in Queens, where he was living in order to save a little cash. He was rushing around, on schedule to catch a train into the city, but he said he had a little time to talk. I asked how his acting was coming along, and he told me he had been cast in "a couple of TV things." nothing big, but he was hanging in and reacquainting himself with his "love for the craft." It was then that I told him about my own experience returning to the stage, about why I had left acting in the first place, my struggles with stage fright and the discoveries I had made along the way. I told him about my breakthrough, how Sue had come to my rescue by telling me I needed to worry about my character instead of the lines. And this led me to the conclusion that I should rely on subtext rather than surface text. And I marveled at the simple idea that some people were just meant to be actors and others were not. I know many actors like Keith who, for one reason or another, leave the stage, but they never really do. They always find a way back. It's like a habit they can't quit, an addiction.

Keith suggested that my latching on to the subtext was merely a way of taking control of my performance, and also had something to do with my work as a director and playwright. Subtext, not text, of the character is what I eventually memorized, and this is because as a playwright, I live in the heads of my characters, so I'm privy to their drives, their desires and wants, expressed and unexpressed. It was safer, easier, and ultimately more beneficial for me to memorize the inner workings of Dorn than the words he chose to present himself to the outside world. Perhaps I would have frozen on stage, as I had done years before, if I had never become a playwright in the intervening years. Having learned the craft of creating characters, I had a tool I didn't have then. I was keenly aware of subtext, and that awareness, that ability to tap into it, saved me, allowed me to confront my fears. So ostensibly, waiting this long was the only way I was going to get through being on stage again.

But there's something more to what Keith said. And it has to do with playing a real person, because we're all, every one of us, not living the life of our words, but the life we live in our imagination. Our desires and dreams drive us to the choices we make. And this is what we should always be aware of. The only way I could ever feel comfortable and authentic with Dorn was if I learned his inner life. Just as the only way I feel comfortable with myself is when I'm aware of and in touch with my inner feelings. Whatever words I choose to express myself do not matter. They are not who I am. We are the sum of our actions. That's what we remember and are remembered for. And, ultimately, it's the only thing that matters in real life and imagined life. Looking at it this way, like Stella Adler once concluded, "The words just don't matter."

At the time I talked to Keith, he was basically starting over. But he had no regrets he said, because he was in a very bad place when he had left acting years ago. Back then, he was only concerned about his successes, how he was perceived by others, becoming a star and getting the next big job. He needed to give all that up, divert his attentions and then return with nothing in order to find the joy he had lost. Acting, now, was a chance to be seen, yes, but it was also a way to immerse himself in a character of another and live life always in the present. There is no future on stage, no past, only now. And living in that "now" is where tranquility, connection, craft, and art exist.

I don't know if I ever found that absolutely when I was performing Dorn, but I have to believe that was where I was headed.

About fifteen minutes into our talk, Keith apologized, we might get cut off. He was on the move, having left his parents house and nearing the train. He was on his way to one of his several day jobs. But he had one last piece of advice. He told me that if I was going to write this book, I should not try to explain too much about my experience searching for meaning in acting, because much of what we all love about theatre lives in a mystery that can never be solved. And never should be solved. There is something inexplicable about the life we live—frightening and exciting at once—a leap in the dark, into the forever unknown. And if theatre is a reflection of life, well, then that's just perfect.

Not a bad thought. But it still leaves me wanting.

ABOUT THE AUTHOR

ERIC SIMONSON—is a director and writer of theatre, film and opera, and an ensemble member of Steppenwolf Theatre. He is the author of the plays *Lombardi, Magic/Bird* and *Bronx Bombers* all of which ran on Broadway, as well as many other plays which have appeared across the country and around the world. He has written for television extensively, and his documentary film *A Note of Triumph* won an Academy Award. He is a graduate of Lawrence University, the artistic director of the Door Kinetic Arts Festival in Wisconsin, and resides in Los Angeles with his wife Sue and son Henry.

[www.ericsimonson.org]

[www.doorkinetic.com]

Printed in the USA
CPSIA information can be obtained
at www.ICGtesting.com
CBHW031627131124
17315CB00025B/686